PowerPoint 2000

Rachel Kirk

TEACH YOURSELF BOOKS

For UK orders: please contact Bookpoint Ltd, 78 Milton Park, Abingdon, Oxon OX14 4TD. Telephone: (44) 01235 400414, Fax: (44) 01235 400454. Lines are open 9.00 – 6.00, Monday to Saturday, with a 24-hour message answering service. E-mail address: orders@bookpoint.co.uk

For USA and Canada orders: please contact NTC/Contemporary Publishing, 4255 West Touhy Avenue, Lincolnwood, Illinois 60646-1975, USA. Telephone: (847) 679 5500, Fax: (847) 679 2494.

Long renowned as the authoritative source for self-guided learning – with more than 40 million copies sold worldwide – the *Teach Yourself* series includes over 200 titles in the fields of languages, crafts, hobbies, business and education.

British Library Cataloguing in Publication Data
A catalogue record for this title is available from the British Library.

Library of Congress Catalog Card Number: On file

First published in UK 1999 by Hodder Headline Plc, 338 Euston Road, London, NW1 3BH

First published in US by NTC/Contemporary Publishing, 4255 West Touhy Avenue, Lincolnwood (Chicago), Illinois 60646-1975 USA.

The 'Teach Yourself' name and logo are registered trade marks of Hodder & Stoughton Ltd. Microsoft®, PowerPoint 2000®, NetMeeting®, NetShow® and Outlook® are registered trademarks or trademarks of Microsoft Corporation.

Typeset by MacDesign, Southampton
Printed in Great Britain for Hodder & Stoughton Educational, a division of Hodder Headline Plc, 338 Euston Road, London NW1 3BH by Cox & Wyman, Reading, Berkshire.

Impression number	10 9 8 7 6 5 4 3 2 1
Year	2005 2004 2003 2002 2001 2000 1999

CONTENTS

ACKNOWLEDGEMENTS

I would like to thank June Pugh and Miriam Pownell for their determined efforts to work through the contents of this book! Without their time and patience life would have been much more stressful. On that note, I would like thank my family for tolerating me being shut away with my computer night and day. I know I pushed their patience to the limit.

PREFACE

This book is written to assist your development and understanding of Microsoft PowerPoint. It is an introduction to the software, offering basic instructions. It is aimed at users with a reasonable understanding of Windows 95 or 98 Operating Systems and Microsoft software, terminology and practices. If you are familiar with any of the Microsoft Office, Works or Publisher applications then you will have noticed that they all operate along similar formats, i.e. they all use drop-down menus, have toolbars, and use the same commands for the general functions such as save, print, page set up. It is only when you start to use commands specific to particular applications that you'll start to see a difference. This is also true of PowerPoint.

This book is written for PowerPoint 2000. If you have a previous version, there may be some differences, but fundamentally the applications will be the same.

It is recommended that you follow the book chapter by chapter so as to gain the most from it. Each chapter will introduce a new topic, or go into greater depth of a related topic and include stand-alone activities relating to the contents of that chapter. By the end of the book you will have the necessary skills and knowledge to create your own first class presentation. There are two projects in the appendix that can be used for practice purposes. Also included at the end of the book is a quick reference guide (giving bullet point steps) to the essential skills needed for creating a slide presentation.

The commands and operations throughout the book will be presented by the use of the menus and toolbars on screen and the mouse in your hand. If there are any jargon words that you're unsure of, then refer to the glossary at the back of the book where they will be explained. The book is written to be as 'user friendly' as possible!

1 | INTRODUCING POWERPOINT

AIMS OF THIS CHAPTER

This chapter introduces PowerPoint and its main functions. We will also look at PowerPoint Wizards and learn how to work with them.

1.1 What is PowerPoint?

PowerPoint is a package which can automate presentations and bring to life the static affairs we've used for so many years. Computerized presentations enable you to impart information with the benefits of sound and animated effects through a projector linked to your computer, or by using the **Pack and Go Wizard** (see section 1.5 and Chapter 11) from another computer. Presentations can also be made on the Internet with each member of the audience at a remote site with interactive capabilities (see Chapter 9).

When using PowerPoint, the presentation itself becomes hassle free. It is impossible to get the slides in the wrong order, upside down or for the carousel to jam. The margin of error is, therefore, reduced.

Presentations can be produced as slide shows, which can be viewed directly from the monitor, through a projector or on the Internet. Speaker's notes can be produced, giving a shot of the slide and prompt notes to support the presenter. Overhead projector (OHP) transparencies can be printed, as can 35 mm slides and handouts for the audience (see Chapter 4).

Like all Microsoft software, PowerPoint is supported by a number of smaller applications. These include WordArt, Draw, Graph 2000 and Organization Chart (see Chapters 6, 7 and 8) and it can be integrated with other Microsoft applications such as Word or Excel.

PowerPoint 2000 is the latest version of the software, and is normally supplied as part of the Office 2000 suite.

1.2 Using PowerPoint

PowerPoint is no different from any other Microsoft product and can be opened in one of three ways:

❶   Double-click on the PowerPoint shortcut button on the Desktop.

❷   Click on the **PowerPoint** button on the Office shortcut bar on the Desktop.

❸   Click on the **Start** button on the Taskbar, point to **Programs** and select **Microsoft PowerPoint**.

Having opened PowerPoint in the appropriate way for your computer the application will have loaded and look like Figure 1.1.

The opening screen for PowerPoint allows you to decide how you want to create a presentation. At this stage, however, we're going to take a tour of the screen so we need to open a blank presentation:

♦   Select *Blank presentation* and click **OK**.

This will enable you to move to the next stage which is to select the type of slide you want to use. Don't worry, we're not going to create a slide just yet, we're using this as a way of getting into the working screen to view it.

♦   Click **OK** again.

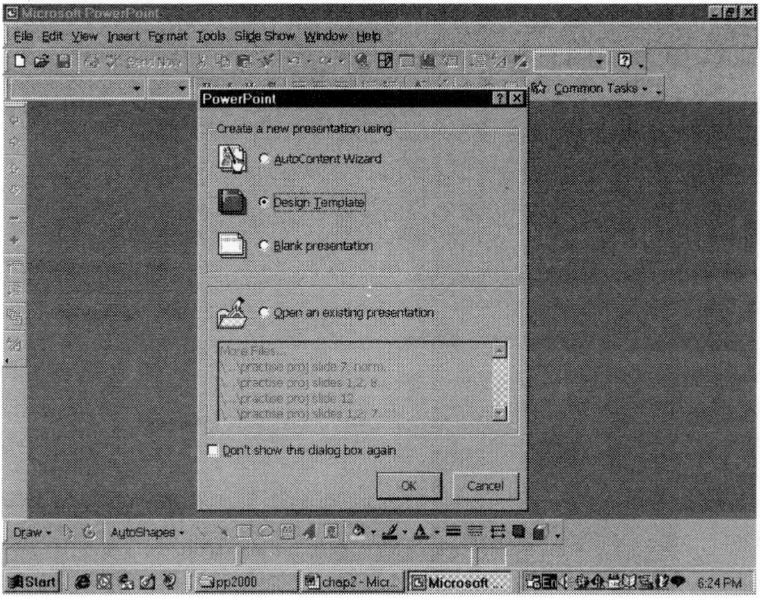

Figure 1.1 The PowerPoint screen when starting to create a new presentation – select Blank presentation and click OK to clear the startup dialog box so that you can see the working screen

1.3 The PowerPoint screen

These are the key elements of the working screen.

Title bar

The Title bar appears at the top of the window and shows the title of the file in which you are working, together with the name of the application being used. It also shows the Maximize, Minimize and Close buttons for the application, used for shrinking or increasing the size of the application window or closing it altogether.

Menu bar

This shows the names of the menus. When clicked upon, a name will reveal a drop-down list of commands and options stored within that menu.

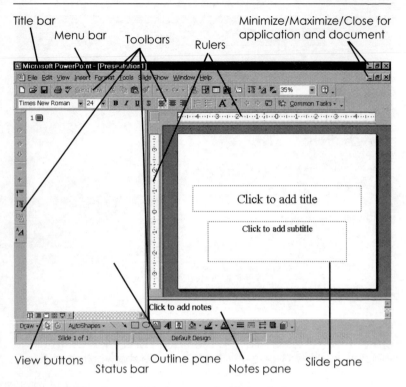

Figure 1.2 The PowerPoint screen in Normal view

The Menu bar also holds the Maximize, Minimize and Close buttons for the document in which you're working, if the document window is maximized.

Toolbars

There are a number of toolbars available in any application. Usually only the two main toolbars are shown: the Standard toolbar and the Formatting toolbar. All the toolbars provide shortcut facilities for carrying out most of the commands found within the drop-down menus.

The others can be opened by clicking on the **View** menu then selecting **Toolbars** and clicking on the toolbar to be opened.

Scroll Bars

These will appear at the bottom and right-hand side of the Outline, Slide and Notes panes whenever they contain more than can be displayed in the available space. Where there are several slides, clicking on the double-headed arrows at the foot of the right-hand scroll bar of the Slide pane will take you to the previous or next slide.

View buttons

The PowerPoint screen has six different display modes, or Views, which you can use at the various stages of creating and checking your presentations (see Chapter 3). You can switch between the most-used Views with the View buttons in the bottom left corner of the screen.

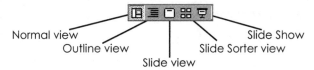

Normal view
Outline view
Slide view
Slide Sorter view
Slide Show

Status bar

This can be found at the bottom of your screen and gives the latest status of the file. It contains information such as the slide number you're working on, the view in which you're working and information about the area of the screen at which your mouse is pointing.

Having looked at the PowerPoint screen we now need to close the file and exit the application.

❶ Open the **File** menu and click **Close**. (You might be asked if you wish to save the changes made to your file. Click **No** as we haven't made any changes.)

❷ Open the **File** menu again and click **Exit** to leave the application.

Or

♦ Close the file and exit in one step by clicking the **Close** button on the application title bar.

Close the application

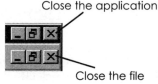

Close the file

1.4 Wizards

Most Microsoft applications offer *wizards*. A wizard is a facility that will do all the work for you – all you have to do is insert the relevant text at the appropriate point. Wizards are useful if you do not want to design your own files but they do take away the opportunity to expand your knowledge base!

As with all wizards, those available in PowerPoint take you through a series of steps and at each you will be asked to make a selection, or answer questions. This is so that the wizard can either put together a presentation based on your specifications or, if you're using Pack and Go Wizard, save the information on to a floppy disk.

Pack and Go Wizard

You can use the Pack and Go Wizard to show your presentation on a different computer. Just follow its steps and the wizard will 'pack up' all the different elements of the presentation that are needed for it to be transferred. These include things such as the fonts used, the clip art, sounds and relevant attached files. If the presentation is being packed to show on a computer which doesn't have PowerPoint installed it will also package the PowerPoint Viewer onto the disk (see Chapter 11).

AutoContent Wizard

The AutoContent Wizard provides an outline presentation for the most commonly used or popular presentations. The wizard offers a range of styles for the presentation, all stored within different categories, for instance Corporate, Projects and Sales/marketing. Some of these can be used over the Internet.

The following activity takes you through the process of creating a very simple presentation using the wizard. It touches briefly on elements of PowerPoint that will be covered in greater detail further on in this book.

❶ Open **PowerPoint**.

❷ At the start-up dialog box, select the **AutoContent Wizard** and click **OK**.

There are three ways to create a new presentation – the AutoContent Wizard is probably the easiest

Or, if you are already working within PowerPoint:

❶ Open the **File** menu.

❷ Select **New**.

❸ Click on the **General** tab (see Figure 1.3)

❹ Double-click on **AutoContent Wizard**.

Either method will bring you to the start of the AutoContent Wizard. You now follow a series of steps, giving the wizard the details it needs to create a presentation for you.

Figure 1.4 shows the first panel that appears in the wizard. On the left is the list of steps you will take to work through the wizard.

♦ Click **Next** or click the box beside **Presentation Type** to progress to the next step of the wizard.

The presentation types cover most of the activities which are commonly the subject of presentations in business. The **All** category shows a list of all the available types. It would probably be wise to decide which category your presentation is in and click on that, then scroll through the options within that category.

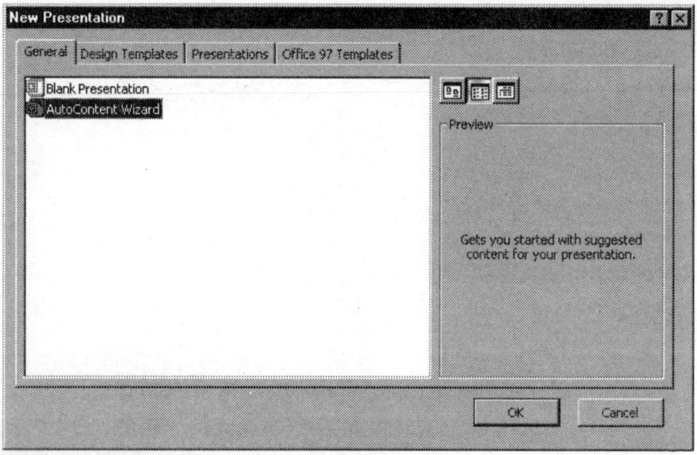

Figure 1.3 Starting from AutoContent Wizard. Notice that you can also start from a template selected from one of the other tabs in this dialog box. We will return to templates in Chapter 2

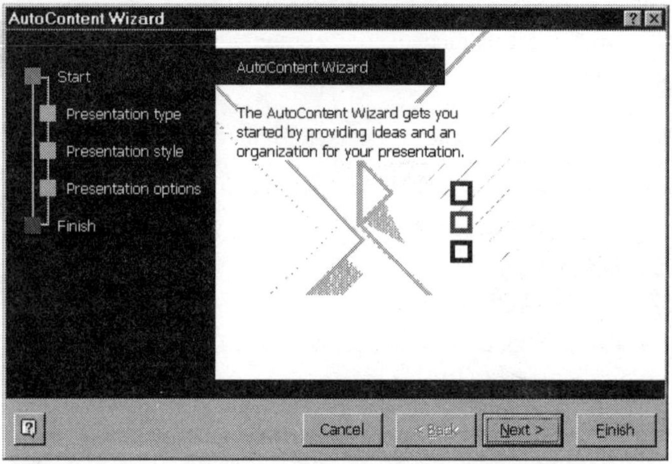

Figure 1.4 The opening panel of AutoContent Wizard – after completing each panel, move on by clicking the Next button or the box by the next item in the list on the left

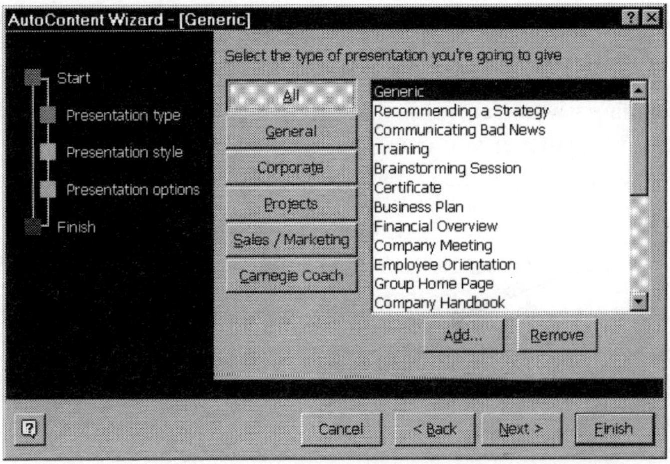

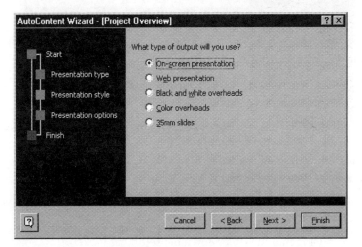

Figure 1.5 Selecting the presentation type

* Open the **Project** category and select *Project overview*.

The style refers to the output format. PowerPoint can be used for on-screen or Web presentations, overhead transparencies or 35 mm slides. Whatever format is used you can produce speaker's notes for the presenter and handouts for the audience (see Chapter 4).

Figure 1.6 Selecting the presentation style

❶   Select the style of output needed.

❷   Move on to the **Next** step.

At this step you can enter the title text, which will go on the first slide.
(It doesn't matter if you chose not to, as it can be added later). The
footer can also be defined now, or left until later (see Chapter 5).

❶   Insert your text into the **Presentation title**, e.g.:
    Presentation Outline

❷   Leave the **Footer** and other options and click **Next**.

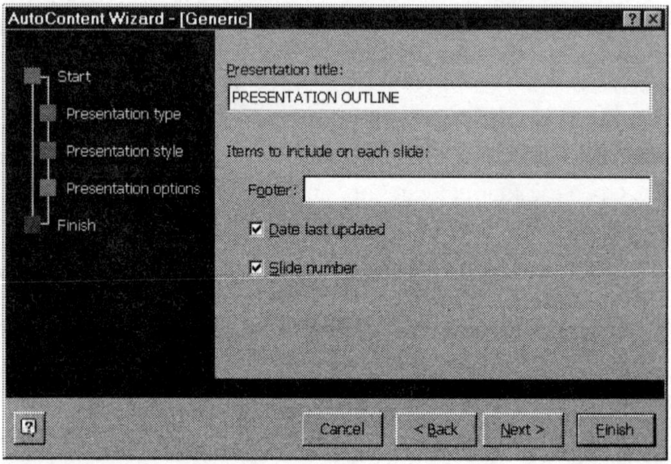

Figure 1.7 Entering the title

♦   At the final step click **Finish** to enable the wizard to cre-
    ate your presentation.

The wizard will create a series of slides for the presentation (the number
will depend on the presentation type that you selected). As the wizard
finishes it closes and returns to the working screen, you will see your
work in Normal view (see Figure 1.9).

Move through the text down the left side of the screen (the *Outline
pane*) either by:

♦   Dragging the slider down the scroll bar.

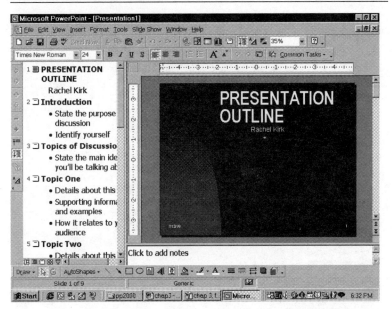

Figure 1.8 The new presentation, opened in Normal view

- ◆ Clicking on the arrow at the bottom of the scroll bar.

- ◆ Clicking the insertion point into the text somewhere and using the arrow keys on the keyboard.

The only slide to contain any of your own text is the first. The rest contain suggestions for what should be covered at that point, and these should be replaced by your own words.

When working with text use the same techniques you would in a word processor. Text can be entered directly into the slide, or in the Outline pane – use whichever you find most convenient.

To insert the relevant text for the others:

❶ Move the insertion point to where the text is to be changed, i.e. **Slide 2 – Ultimate goal of project**.

❷ Select and delete the existing text.

❸ Type in the text: **To outline contents of the presentation**

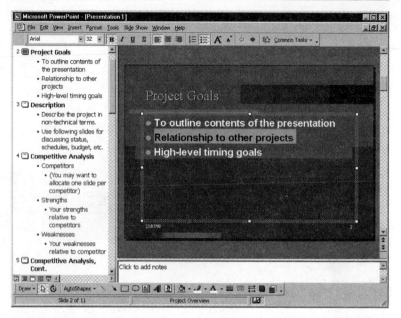

Figure 1.9 The second line of text has been selected and is about to be replaced

Having reached the appropriate slide, click into the line of text to be changed. You'll notice a box will appear around the text, this is called a *placeholder* and the *insertion point* is situated on the line you selected, within the placeholder.

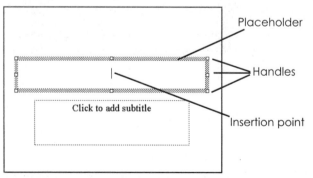

Figure 1.10 Placeholder and insertion point

These steps can be repeated for each line of each slide. Change the text in slide 3 (the slide number will be visible on the Status bar).

❶ Move through to slide 3

❷ Click on the line Describe the project...

❸ Delete the contents and type in the new line of text:
   The conference will take the form of a workshop

You can continue in this manner to change all the text in your presentation.

It is also possible to edit the slides whilst viewing them, as they will appear by opening Slide view:

◆ Click on the **Slide view** button at the bottom left of your screen:

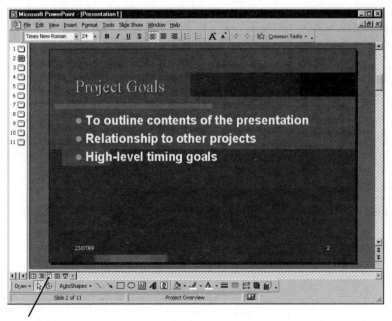

Slide view

Figure 1.11 Slide view gives you more room to work on a slide

The screen will change to show the selected slide, and collapse the outline of the presentation into a simple list of numbered slide icons.

- ◆ To edit a slide, move to the correct one by using the right scroll bar slider or double arrows – click on the downward double arrow to move to the next slide, click on the upward double arrow to move to the previous one.

When you have finished, save the file – open the **File** menu, select **Save As** and give it a suitable filename.

The **Wizard** style used in this practice task is a very simple one and only uses a limited selection of the features available in PowerPoint. We will, however, be examining others, such as clip art, sounds and colour schemes, further on in this book. All of these other features can also be used in **AutoContent Wizard** presentations.

SUMMARY

In this chapter we have discussed:

✓ The uses of PowerPoint.

✓ The PowerPoint screen.

✓ The use of wizards in PowerPoint

✓ How the AutoContent Wizard can get you started quickly on a new presentation.

✓ Entering text into a slide.

PREPARATION

It is always worth sketching out your presentation on paper before putting it onto the computer. Decide on the number of slides, write out the text for each and include rough outlines of the graphics. If you create the presentation on the computer as you go, it will tend to become a bit confused and not as professional and clear as you want.

2 | TEMPLATES AND AUTOLAYOUT

AIMS OF THIS CHAPTER

In this chapter we will look at the differences between working with a blank presentation and a template, and learning which will suit our situation better. We will also look at Autolayout slides, and how these are used.

2.1 Templates

When working with any computer application you might not be aware but you are in fact working in a *template*. Even the blank document that is opened up on loading your word processor, spreadsheet, database, etc. is a template. It has been predesigned with a default font, font size, margins and sometimes headers and footers, to meet the needs of an average document. These preset elements make up a template.

When selecting a template in PowerPoint you are choosing a background style for your slides, together with the font and formatting styles thought to be most appropriate. In most cases, unlike AutoContent Wizard, it doesn't create a series of slides.

In PowerPoint there are a number of different templates available to you. They are all reached through **Design Templates** option in the startup dialog box, or through the **File – New** command, which opens the **New Presentation** dialog box. There, on the **General** tab, you will also find *Blank Presentation*, which has a plain white background and the default font styles. (You can also start with a blank presentation by clicking **New** ◲ on the Standard toolbar.)

The advantage of a blank presentation is that you can put your own mark on it, setting up your own colour scheme and text formats.

General also contains the *AutoContent Wizard*.

The **Design Templates** offer the same facility as Blank Presentation but provides a range of different design schemes to meet different user needs, e.g. *Artsy*, *Blends* or *Blueprint*. A template selected from here only creates one slide.

The **Presentations** work in a very similar way to the AutoContent Wizard. A template from here, e.g. *Company Meeting*, will not only have a colour scheme and formatting predesigned, but it will consist of a series of slides. Each of these is already set up with placeholders for text and clip art or other graphics where your details and images can be inserted. The only difference between Presentations and the AutoContent Wizard is that a Presentations template doesn't take you through a series of steps to customize it.

If PowerPoint 2000 has been installed over a previous version of the software, you may have an *Office 97 Templates* tab. Most of these options are also present, in newer editions, on the Design Templates and Presentations tabs.

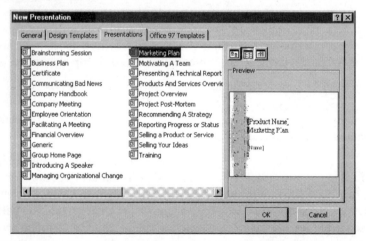

Figure 2.1 The **New Presentation** dialog box, open at the **Presentations** tab. Use the Preview to help you select one

It is also possible to create your own template so that your formatting can be reused in other presentations (see Chapter 12).

2.2 New slides

After choosing a blank presentation or a template your next step will be the New Slide dialog box to define the layout. This offers a selection of *Autolayouts* – predesigned layouts for a slide. In other words, a range of slide designs which contain space for clip art, etc. for a number of different scenarios.

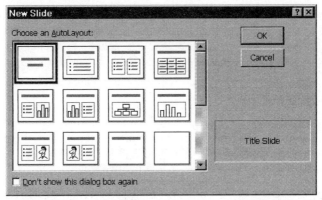

Figure 2.2 The **New Slide** dialog box

It is in the New Slide dialog box that you can select any combination of placeholders for the various elements of your slide. It is also possible to rearrange the placeholders as necessary, or delete them to insert your own.

Amongst the selection of Autolayout slides is a blank slide which, if you wish, can be used for every slide in your presentation. Using this one gives you the opportunity to put your own kind of placeholder in wherever you require.

Don't feel too restricted by the pre-set choices as placeholders can be moved and resized easily, as you will see while working through this book.

2.3 Using Presentation templates

So now we're going to try a couple of things out. First of all we are
going to create a presentation using a Presentation template.

❶   Start PowerPoint if necessary.

❷   Select **Design Templates** and click **OK**.

❸   Bring the **Presentations** tab to the front.

❹   Select *Project overview*.

❺   Click on **OK**.

Now the slides are open on the computer, in Normal view, and you can
start entering the necessary text. For instance, in the first slide:

❶   Click onto *Project Overview* in the main slide area – note
      how the placeholder appears around the text.

❷   Delete the text contained within the placeholder and type in:
      Presentation to Conference

◆   Don't press **[Enter]**after typing in the heading – it will
      give you a line space which you don't want.

❸   Click onto *Project Name* (the placeholder will appear
      around all three bulleted items).

❹   Delete the contents of the first line and type in:
      Presentation for National Teaching Conference

❺   Staying within this placeholder, move to the next line and
      replace the contents with the company name*:*
      Teaching Resources Ltd

PRACTICAL EXERCISES

Sample text and graphics has been suggested for all of
the exercises in this book. If you want to replace all or any
of this with your own material, please feel free to do so.
The important thing is to work through the activities – the
content is not important at this stage.

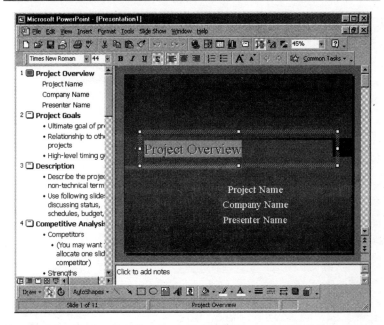

Figure 2.3 Replacing the template text – note that the place-holder goes around blocks of related text, not just single lines

   ❻   Move the insertion point to the last line, delete the contents and key in your name.

Now work through the other slides and make changes to the text so that you get the feel of using a presentation template.

Saving a presentation

Presentations should be saved early and often. This way, if there is a power failure or a system crash you won't lose much work.

The first time you save the presentation, you will have to choose the folder to store it in and give it a name. Subsequent saves will overwrite the older version on the disk, unless you use the Save As option and give the new version a different name. You might want to do this, for example, if you are producing several versions before deciding which looks best..

❶   Open the **File** menu.

❷   Select **Save** (or **Save As** to save a new version of an exist-
    ing presentation) to open the Save As dialog box.

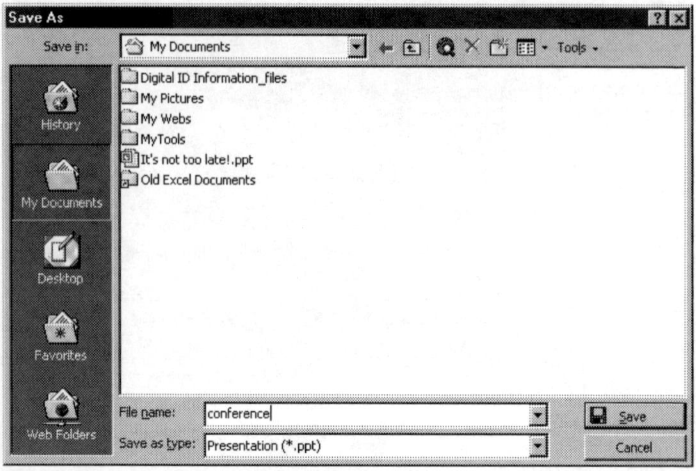

Figure 2.4 The Save As dialog box

❸   Change the folder and edit the file name if you wish – the
    first slide's title will be offered as the name.

❹   Click **Save**.

◆   To resave a presentation, click **Save** 🔲 on the Standard
    toolbar.

2.4 Using Design templates

As an alternative to Presentation templates, you can use Design templates. These simply set up the background colour scheme and text
formats, and not a set of predefined slides. This will give more free-
dom for your personal input and own choice of slides at the stages you
want them to come.

❶   If you are loading PowerPoint, select **Design template**
    from the dialog box, then click on **OK**.

Or

❷   If you are already in PowerPoint, open the **File** menu and click **New**.

❸   Whichever of the above steps you used, you will arrive at the **New Presentation** dialog box. On the **Design templates** tab, select a template, e.g. *Soaring* and click **OK.**

You will now have the New Slide dialog box on the screen. The presentation will need a **title** slide.

❹   Click on the first option, *Title Slide*, to select it, then click **OK**.

The screen will change to show you the first slide, displayed in Normal view. At the moment the slide contains two boxes, or placeholders, where you can insert your text. The top one is the *title placeholder* and the lower one is the *subtitle placeholder*. Each has been preset with text formatting so that whatever you type in will appear in a font, font size and alignment considered suitable for a title or subtitle.

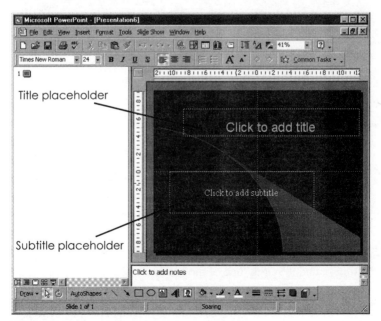

Figure 2.5 Placeholders in a new Title slide

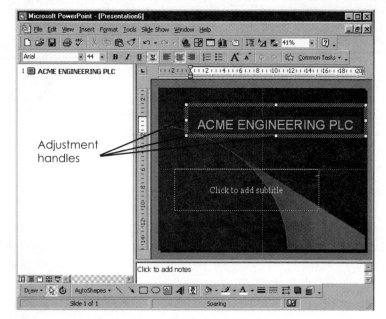

Figure 2.6 Selected placeholders

♦ Now insert your text into the title placeholder and sub-title placeholder. The title of the presentation is:

Acme Engineering plc

To insert the title text:

❶ Click into the **title placeholder**. The insertion point appears, flashing, in the centre.

❷ Type the title into the title placeholder.

❸ Now click on the subtitle placeholder and type in:

Staff Training Programme

It is possible to move a placeholder, resize it or change its shape by selecting it, and dragging one of the handles.

♦ Point at a handle, to get the double-headed arrow ↔, then hold the left mouse button down and drag the handle, in, out, up or down to change the placeholder's shape.

You can move it to a different position by pointing at one of its *sides*, not a handle. When you get the four arrow-headed  hold the left button down and drag it to the point at which it should be situated.

    ◆   Position the subtitle so that the placeholder is on the right of the slide, below the title, and made narrower so that it takes up two lines as shown in Figure 2.7.

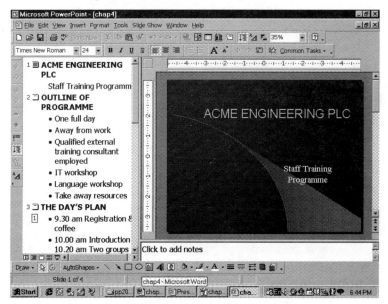

Figure 2.7 Repositioned placeholders

It's time to add some more slides. After all, one slide does not a presentation make! The slides to be added are:

        Slide 2 Bulleted list

        Slide 3 Two columns

        Slide 4 Bulleted list

To insert a new slide into the presentation after the existing slide:

  ❶ Open the **Insert** menu.

❷ Select **New Slide**.

Or

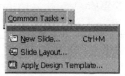

◆ Click on **Common Tasks** on the Formatting toolbar and select **New Slide**.

❸ At the **New Slide** dialog box, select the bulleted list for
Slide 2 and click **OK**.

❹ Repeat this process for each of the other slides in the above
list, to give a total of four in the presentation.

❺ Save the presentation as *acme*.

Slide 2

Now you need to insert the text for slide 2.

❶ Click twice on the **Previous slide** button on the vertical
scroll bar on the right of the screen to return to slide 2.

❷ In Slide 2 select the title placeholder and key in the title:
Outline of programme

❸ In the *bulleted list* placeholder, key in the list of details
about the training programme as shown below:
• One full day
• Away from work
• Qualified external training consultant employed
• IT workshop
• Language workshop
• Take away resources

Save the work done so far, to update the file with the changes and
additions made.

❶ Open the **File** menu and select **Save**.

Or

◆ Click the **Save** button ▦ on the Standard toolbar

Slide 3

Use the **Next slide** button on the vertical scroll bar to move to the third slide and fill in the following title details in the title placeholders:

The day's plan

This timetable should go into the two columnar lists. The morning's timetable should go on the left and the afternoon's on the right.

9.30 am	Registration & coffee
10.00 am	Introduction
10.20 am	Two groups to discuss day's plans
10.30 am	Two workshops
11.30 am	Coffee break
11.45 am	Resume workshops
1.00 pm	Break for lunch
2.00 pm	Swop workshops
3.15 pm	Tea break
3.30 pm	Resume
4.30 pm	Finish, rejoin as one group for review of day
5.00 pm	Go home!

When you've finished with this slide, save your work and then move onto the fourth slide. Use the **Next slide** button again.

Slide 4

This is another bulleted list. Enter this title in the appropriate place:

Expectations of day

The contents of the bulleted list are:

- Staff to be brought up to date with new IT systems
- Staff given opportunity to update European language skills for new business
- Opportunity for team building within the business
- Business employing staff who will be better prepared for working in an international market

Save your work. You now have a simple presentation. Well done!

2.5 Closing and opening presentations

Documents (and applications) should always be closed down properly when you have finished with them – never just turn off the computer! A proper close down ensures that your work is safe.

❶   Open the **File** menu and select **Close**.

Or

◆   Click the presentation's **Close** button

If the presentation has been edited since the last save, you will be prompted to save it now. Do so if you want to keep the edits.

When you want to view or work on your presentation again, you must open it.

❶   Open the **File** menu and select **Open.**

❷   From the **Look in** box select the appropriate folder.

❸   From the list of files click on the required name.

❹   Click **Open**.

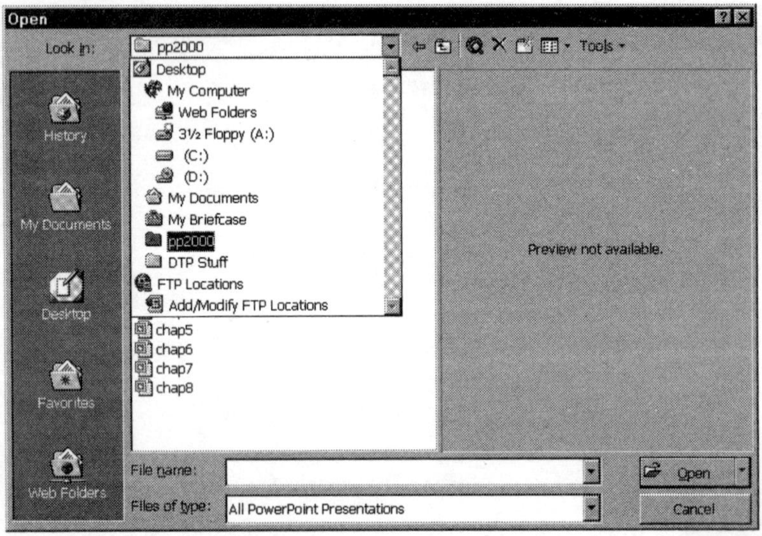

Figure 2.8 The Open dialog box

SUMMARY

In this chapter we have covered the following:

✓ The concept of templates and how they work.

✓ The different types of templates.

✓ Choosing an autolayout at the New Slide dialog box.

✓ Simple manipulation of text and the use of placeholders in our work.

✓ Closing and opening presentation files.

3 | VIEWING WORK

AIMS OF THIS CHAPTER

In this chapter we will be looking at the different view facilities available in PowerPoint, and which one is best suited to your particular need or the task in hand.

3.1 Viewing your work

Whilst working in PowerPoint you have the option of viewing your work in six different ways:

- Normal view
- Outline view
- Slide view
- Slide Sorter view
- Slide Show
- Notes Page view

Usually you will find that when loading PowerPoint it opens into Normal view. This or Slide view are the two usual views in which to work. The purpose of the different views is to help you whilst creating the presentation. They enable you to see and design the whole slide on the screen (Slide view), work on the text and notes whilst also viewing the slide (Normal view), change and edit just the text (Outline view), view all the slides on one screen and rearrange the order, delete or insert new slides (Slide Sorter view), view and edit, or insert text and data for speaker notes (Notes Page view) or to view the slide show to assess its progression (Slide Show).

By opening the **View** menu you can switch between four of the views, Normal, Notes Page, Slide Sorter and Slide Show. To switch between all of the views, except Notes Pages view, you can click on the buttons at the lower left corner of the PowerPoint window:

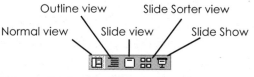

3.2 Normal view

The screenshot below shows the Normal view screen when a new file started, using Blank Presentation.

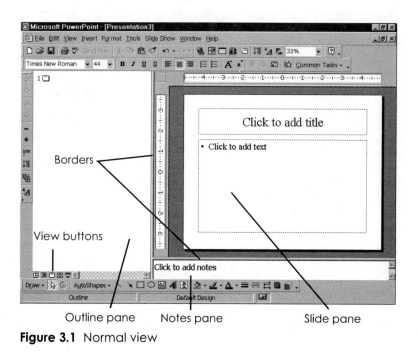

Figure 3.1 Normal view

Normal and Slide view are the usual windows in which to work. By using Normal view you are able to work in three different areas:

- **Outline pane**, enabling you to edit or insert text.

- **Notes pane**, which provides an area where the speaker's notes can be included.

- **Slide pane** within which you can also edit text, insert or manipulate graphics and add any effects.

It is possible to reduce or increase the size of each pane by dragging the border in or out with the mouse. Dragging the right-hand border of the Outline pane will make this pane larger and the Slide pane smaller. Dragging the top border of the Notes pane, will increase its size while the Slide pane decreases.

To drag a border point at it with the mouse, hold the left button down and when the ◀‖▶ cursor appears, drag in the appropriate direction.

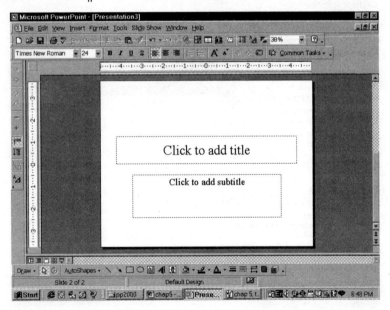

Figure 3.2 Slide view

3.3 Slide view

By changing the view to Slide view you will notice that the PowerPoint window shows only the slide and its formatting. Within this view you can work on the slide, adding and removing text, graphics, sounds, animations and hyperlinks that will affect the individual slide or the whole presentation. You will not see the Outline pane or the Notes pane in this view.

3.4 Outline view

When using Outline view or the Outline pane in Normal view, you will see a draft outline of the text from each slide in the presentation, without any graphics or other effects. You can work in Outline view, entering text from scratch by working with a blank presentation or starting with a template or AutoContent Wizard.

Outline pane   Slide pane

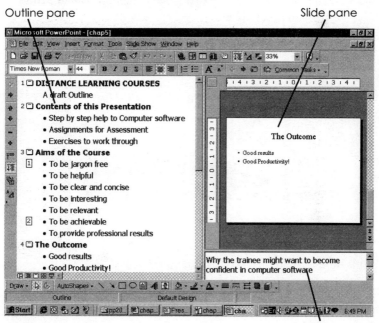

Notes pane

Figure 3.3 Outline view shows the text more clearly

In Outline view, the screen is again divided into three: the text is seen in the Outline pane, the layout of the slide in miniature in the Slide pane and any notes you have made in the Notes pane. As in Normal view, panes can be resized by dragging the borders in, out, up or down.

If there is text in the slides before you turn to Outline view, the title of each slide appears alongside a number and an icon. The icon depicts a slide and the number indicates its place in the order of the presentation.

If there is no text in the slide, then the number and icon will have nothing alongside them.

- To enter data into a slide in Outline view click alongside its icon and key in the appropriate text.

- To move down to the next line of a title placeholder hold down **[Shift]** and press **[Enter]**.

- To move into the next text placeholder hold down **[Control]** and press **[Enter]**.

- To move to the next slide use the arrow keys on the keyboard to move up or down, or move the insertion point with the mouse.

When working in Outline view you will also have an Outling toolbar:

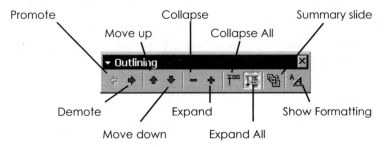

If this toolbar is not displayed, turn it on:

- Open the **View** menu, select **Toolbars** and click **Outline**.
Or
- Point the mouse into a blank area on the open toolbars, click with the right mouse button and select **Outline**.

When using text only in slides it is quicker and more efficient to work within Outline view as you can see the contents of each slide on one screen. By using the various buttons on the toolbar you can move the individual lines of text up and down within a slide or to a different slide; you can move whole slides around, insert or remove slides, or, if needed only show the title line of each slide. Examples are shown later in this chapter (see section 3.8).

Outline view doesn't normally show the font and paragraph formatting that the slide contains. This can be turned on by clicking the **Show Formatting** button on the Outlining toolbar.

3.5 Adding notes

In Normal or Outline view

Notes can be added to either Normal or Outline view for use by the speaker, as prompts for the presentation. These can be printed on their own or as part of a printout showing the slide the notes refer to (see Chapter 4).

- ◆   To add notes simply click the insertion point into the notes pane in either view and type in the necessary text.

In Notes Page view

By adding notes into Notes Page view you are also able to add graphics or Drawing objects which might be useful to the speaker for emphasing points or as a prompt.

- ◆   To open Notes Page view, open the **View** menu and select **Notes Page**.

- ◆   To move between slides in this view simply click on the double-headed arrows on the right-hand scroll bar, as you would in Slide view.

Text is entered into the notes placeholder, exactly as you have previously entered text in the slides. Select the placeholder, position the insertion point and type.

- To place a graphic in this placeholder follow the procedure for inserting a graphic or Drawing object into the
  slide itself (see Chapter 6).

3.6 Slide Sorter view

Slide Sorter view is useful when you've finished putting together your
presentation and want to see all the slides together, in miniature, on
one screen. This might be to ensure that they follow on smoothly, that
they are consistent or that the order is correct. Whilst in Slide Sorter
view you have the facility to move slides around, delete them or insert
a new slide at any point required.

You can also add and check *Timings* and *Animated Transitions* between slides as well as preview these effects (see Chapter 10).

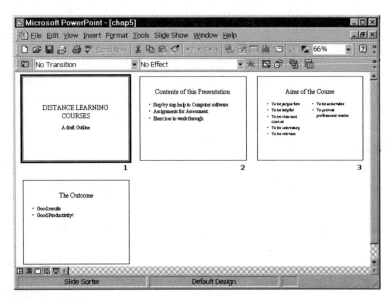

Figure 3.4 Slide Sorter view

3.7 Slide Show view

There are a number of ways of viewing a slide show created on PowerPoint (see Chapter 11). Here though we are concentrating on using the Slide Show view. This can be accessed through the View menu or by clicking on the Slide Show button.

By viewing the presentation this way you can see the whole show on the computer monitor, or the computer can be linked to a projector and shown to a larger audience, or it can be used to show the presentation over the Internet, for instance as part of an on-line meeting (see Chapter 9). You are able to move easily backwards or forwards between slides by using the arrow keys or the mouse, and when you have run through the whole presentation the screen will revert to the view being used before Slide Show view was selected.

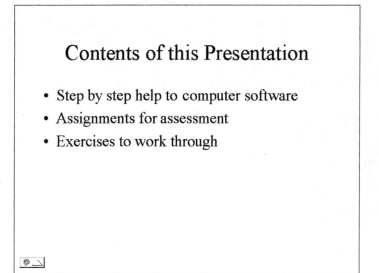

Figure 3.5 Slide Show view

If at any a point you want to stop the presentation and return to the alternative screen view, press **[Escape]**, and if you need to go back to a previous slide click with the right mouse button and select **Previous** from the drop-down menu.

TIP!

Always put a blank slide in at the end of a presentation so that you don't suddenly find your PowerPoint screen being shown on a projector in front of the audience!

3.8 Effective use of the views

Ideally in PowerPoint you would use all the view options in combination. Use Normal view to create slides, insert text and notes; Outline view to edit and reorganize text and slides; Slide view to manipulate Draw objects, clipart, graphics, etc.; Slide Sorter view to change the order of slides; Notes Page view to expand on the speaker's notes; and finally Slide Show view to present the finished product.

So that you can get an idea of how they would all work together we're going to work through a basic presentation of four slides and use the different views to create and manipulate the presentation.

❶   Start PowerPoint and create a new file using *Blank presentation*. From the **New Slide** dialog box select a title slide.

❷   Insert three more slides: a bulleted list slide, a two column text slide and a second bulleted list slide.

Slide 1

❶   Return to the first slide, make sure you're in Normal view. If you're not, click on the Normal view button 🔳.

❷   Enter the title of the slide into the title placeholder:
      Distance learning courses

❸   Click into the subtitle placeholder and type:
      A Draft Outline

❹   In the notes pane add a note:
      Presenter should explain that this is a draft for the final presentation which is to be given next month.

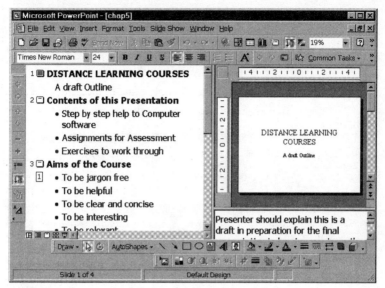

Figure 3.6 The first slide with notes added

Slide 2

❶ Move on to Slide 2 and type in the title placeholder:

Contents of this presentation

❷ Move the insertion point to the text placeholder and insert the following bulleted list:

♦ **Step by step help to computer software**

♦ **Exercises to work through**

♦ **Assignments for assessment**

Slide 3

❶ Move to Slide 3 and key in the title:

Aims of the course

❷ Key in the following into the first column:

♦ **To be jargon free**

♦ **To be helpful**

♦ **To be clear and concise**

❸ The following should be inserted into the second column:
- ◆ To be workable
- ◆ To be achievable
- ◆ To provide professional results

❹ Notes should be added to the note pane to the effect that:
These aims are what the tutors feel are important

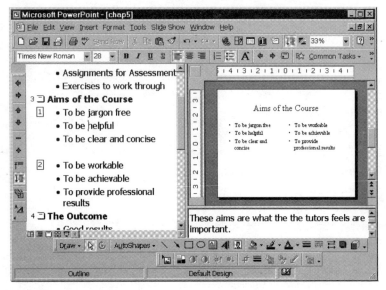

Figure 3.7 Slide 3 uses a two-column display

Slide 4

❶ In Slide 4 add the title:
The Outcome

❷ Add the text:
- ◆ Good results
- ◆ Good productivity!

❸ The notes to be inserted here should be:
Why the trainee might want to become confident in using computer software.

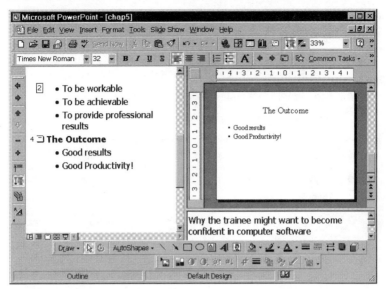

Figure 3.8 Slide 4 with its notes

Click the **Slide view** button ▭ to switch into Slide view and check the appearance of each slide. If you see any typing errors, correct them, then save the file.

Editing text

There are changes that need to be made to the text in the slides and the simplest way to see this clearly is to work in Outline view.

* Change to **Outline view** and position the insertion point into Slide 3. Make the following changes to this slide.

To add new text, e.g. a new line in the first column:

❷ Position the insertion point at the end of the last line in the first column.

❸ Press **[Enter]** to insert a new point

❹ Type in the text:
   To be relevant

To change text, e.g. replace the word 'workable' with 'interesting':

❶ In the second column, delete '**workable**' and type '**interesting**', or double-click it to highlight the word and then type – the new text will replace the highlighted word.

❷ Move to Slide 4 and change '**Good productivity**' to '**More business**'.

To change the order of contents, e.g. in Slide 2, the third point, '**Assignments for assessment**' should be positioned second.

❶ Position the insertion point at the start of the line to be moved.

❷ Click on the **Move up** button on the Outlining toolbar.

Or

♦ Highlight the line and drag it to where it should go.

❸ Save the presentation.

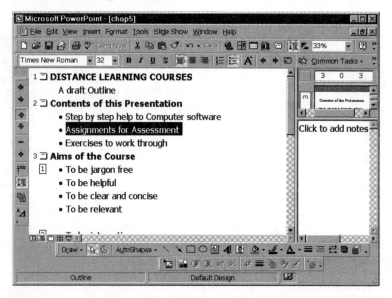

Figure 3.9 Adjusting the order of text items in Outline view

Rearranging the order of slides

The slides need to be rearranged as Slide 3 *'Aims of the course'* should come before Slide 2.

It is easier to move slides around in Slide Sorter view than any other because you can see all the slides on screen. The slides appear in miniature, and the selected one has a thicker line around it, see Figure 3.10.

The simplest way to reposition a slide, is to drag it.

❶ Select the slide to be repositioned.

❷ Hold down the left mouse button and point to where you want the slide to go – a thin line will appear between the nearest slides.

❸ Release the mouse button and the slide will jump into its new place.

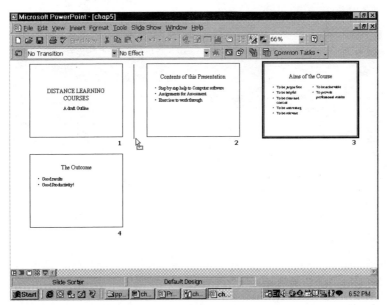

Figure 3.10 Moving a slide in Slide Sorter view – notice the thin indicator line above the mouse pointer

Slides can also be rearranged in Outline view. It is the same process as moving individual lines of text within a slide:

   ❶ Select a slide by clicking its icon.

   ❷ Use the **Move up/Move down** buttons on the Outlining toolbar to move the slide. (This will move the slide up or down one line at a time.)

To move a whole slide in one go:

   ❶ Collapse the appearance of the slide so that only the title lines of slides are shown – click the **Collapse all** button 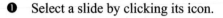 on the toolbar.

   ❷ Select the slide to be moved and again use the **Move up/ Move down** buttons to reposition the slide.

Alternatively, highlight the slide (by clicking on the icon) and drag the slide to its new location.

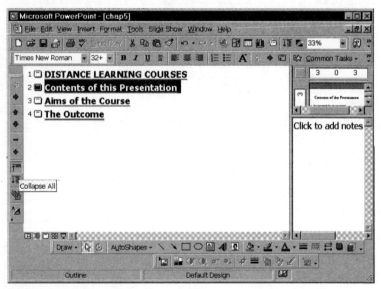

Figure 3.11 Adjusting the order of slides in Outline view

Finishing off

Two more slides need to be added to the presentation. Slide 5 will be the end of the presentation and contain the title of the book. Slide 6 will remain blank so that the presentation can finish on a blank screen rather than reverting to the working screen.

To insert these extra slides return to the Outline view:

❶ Position the insertion point at the end of the last line of text on Slide 4.

❷ Hold down **[Control]**and press **[Enter]** for a new slide to be added (Note that when slides are added this way they take the same format as the slide from which they were created, in this case Slide 4.)

❸ Repeat the above process to insert a Slide 6.

❹ In Slide 5 type in the following in the title placeholder:
    Distance learning courses

❺ Leave the other placeholder empty.

❻ Don't enter anything into the last slide as this is going to be the end of the presentation.

❼ Save the presentation and return to the first slide.

Finally, our presentation is complete! It is time to view it.

3.9 Viewing a presentation

Always check your presentation in Slide Show view, as this is how others will see it.

To go into Slide Show view:

◆ Open the **View** menu and select **Slide Show view**.

Or

◆ Click the **Slide Show view** button .

You'll notice that the title bar, menu bar, toolbars and so forth are all removed from your screen which is filled by the slide.

To move on to the next slide:

- Press **[Pg Up]**, the **Up** arrow key, **[Space bar]** or **[Enter]**

Or

- Click the left mouse button.

To go back to the previous slide:

- Press **[Pg Dn]** or the **Down** arrow key.

Or

- Click the right mouse button and select **Previous** from the shortcut menu.

To leave the presentation at any time:

- Press **[Escape]**.

Or

- Right-click and select **End Show** from the shortcut menu.

| Next |
| Previous |
| Go |
| Meeting Minder... |
| Speaker Notes |
| Pointer Options |
| Screen |
| Help |
| End Show |

SUMMARY

In this chapter we have covered:

✓ the different types of view options available in PowerPoint.

✓ How to insert, edit and move text on a slide.

✓ How to rearrange the order of slides.

✓ How to check your pressentation in Slide Show view.

4 | PRINTING IN POWERPOINT

AIMS OF THIS CHAPTER

In this chapter we will look at the different print options available with PowerPoint 2000, and how to produce print outs of slides.

4.1 Different types of printouts

As the presentation is most likely going to be shown as slides, through the computer, one way or another it is not necessary to produce colour printouts, although this can be done.

The printouts are usually supporting material for the speaker or audience and only need to be there as a reminder of the full colour images shown on a large screen, or computer monitor.

You can, therefore, indicate whether or not you want the printouts to appear as **grayscale** or **pure black and white**.

♦ If the slides contain some dense colour or graphics then it might be wise to print using grayscale. If you select black and white then it will appear as solid black on the printout which is difficult to read as well as being expensive on ink.

4.2 Print output

You can print slides onto any medium that your printer can manage, usually paper or overhead projector transparencies. You can also create a presentation to print onto 35 mm slides but these will need to be printed by a special print bureau.

*   If you're working with a US version of Windows 98 operating system you can print 35 mm slides, posters and display prints by sending your file electronically to Genigraphics. Follow the instructions in the Genigraphics Wizard. (See the PowerPoint Help for more information).

4.3 Print Preview

Before printing, you can preview the slides in *pure black and white* or *grayscale* to establish which is going to give the better output.

To preview in grayscale:

*   Click the **Preview** [image] button on the Standard toolbar.

To preview in pure black and white:

*   Hold down **[Shift]** and click the **Preview** button [image].

When previewing if you find that a particular element is too dark for the printout, you want to highlight something, or the greys are too close for the details to be seen properly, it is possible to make adjustments so that the object is clearer. The adjustments only affect the printed image, not the slide, that retains its original colours.

To adjust the grey/black and white display of elements:

❶   Go into grayscale or black and white preview mode.

❷   Select the element – hold **[Shift]** while you click on elements if you want to select more than one.

❸   Right-click on a selected element, point to **Black and White** and click on a colouring option (see Figure 4.1).

Greyscale/Black and White Preview

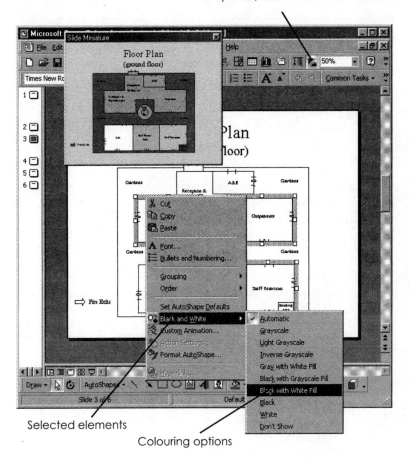

Selected elements

Colouring options

Figure 4.1 Adjusting the display before printing in greyscale or black and white – if the Slide Miniature display gets in your way, click its **Close** button

4.4 Printer Setup

If you open the **File** menu and select **Print...** the Print dialog box will open on your screen.

This is divided into three main sections:

- Printer
- Print range
- Print what

Printer

The **Printer** section will give the name of your default printer. This can be changed if necessary by clicking on the drop-down arrow on the **Printer** box and selecting a different one.

By clicking the **Properties** button in this section you will be presented with details of the settings of the printer. These vary in layout and appearance, depending upon the printer, but all have certain common features, e.g. **Paper size** and **Orientation** (landscape or portrait), how the paper feeds through the printer and colour options of the printer.

The **Orientation** will be set automatically, following the **Page setting** for the file (see Chapter 5).

Print range

The **Print range** section facilitates the printing of the whole file or certain slides within it.

- By requesting **All** the slides, the whole file will print.
- If you select **Current slide** the slide that is up on your screen will be printed.
- The **Selection** option will be available if you have previously selected one or more slides.
- Pick **Slides** if you wish to specify which slides to print. List the numbers of slides, separating with commas or a dash to set a range, e.g. 1, 2, 5 or 1–4, 6, 8, 9–11.

Finally in this section you should state how many copies of the print-out you require. The box will normally show 1 but you can enter any number or click on the arrows alongside it to set the number.

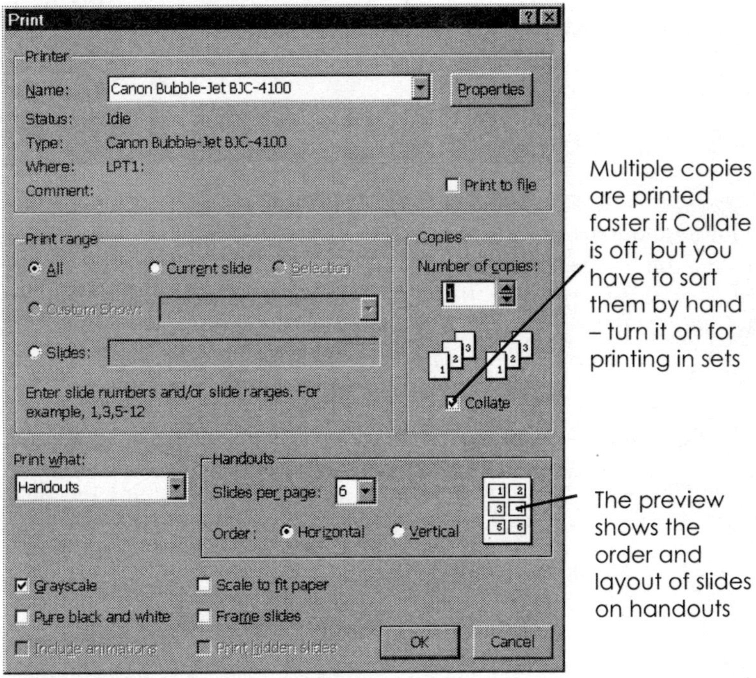

Multiple copies are printed faster if Collate is off, but you have to sort them by hand – turn it on for printing in sets

The preview shows the order and layout of slides on handouts

Figure 4.2 The Print dialog box

Print What

The third section of the print dialog box asks for information about what you're going to print.

In the **Print what:** box you have a choice of different printouts – Slides, Handouts, Notes Pages, or Outline view. If you request Handouts you then need to state how many per page, 2, 3, 4, 6 or 9, and whether to arrange them in vertical or horizontal order.

If the output is to a black and white printer, you should set the printout to grayscale or pure black and white. If you don't the colours will be converted to greys by your printer, rather than by PowerPoint.

There are two last little options here:

- Scale to print will reduce slides, if needed, to fit onto the paper

- Frame slides will add a thin border around the slides, hand-outs or notes pages when they are printed.

4.5 Printing practice

Open one of the presentations that you created earlier – preferably one with a coloured background or that includes a graphic in it. Before asking the printer to print the file you should look at it through **Print preview** to decide whether **grayscale** or **pure black and white** is going to be better.

❶ Go to a slide with a coloured background or graphic.

❷ Click the **Preview** button to see the grayscale quality.

The **print preview** button is a **toggle** button, to return to the file click back on it.

Now check the black and white image:

❶ Hold down **[Shift]** and click the **Preview** button .

- Notice how the button caption now shows '**pure black and white preview**, not **grayscale preview**, as previously.

As you're working mainly with light colours and text it will be better to print using the **black and white print** mode.

Preview

[Shift] and Preview

To adjust the grayscale so that an element's details are clearer:

❶ Click on the object with the right mouse button to open the shortcut menu.

❷ From the shortcut menu point at **Black and white**.

♦ From the list of options select the one that helps show the details most clearly.

Now to print the file!

4.6 Multiple printouts

We need a printout as a handout which will be given to each member of the audience.

❶ Open the **File** menu.

❷ Select **Print**.

❸ In the **Print What** section click on the drop-down arrow and select **Handouts**.

❹ In **Handouts** to the right, specify the number of slide shots per page, e.g. 3.

❺ Specify to print in **Pure Black and White**.

❻ Click **OK** to print.

To do a printout for the speaker's reference:

❶ Open the **File** menu.

❷ Select **Print**.

❸ In **Print What**, select **Notes Page**.

❹ Select **Pure Black and White**.

❺ Click **OK**.

Alternatively, you can print the view that is open on your screen by clicking the **Print** button 🖨 on the toolbar.

When printing speaker's notes you will find that each slide and its accompanying notes takes a whole sheet. This includes a view of the slide, the notes included and the slide number at the bottom of the sheet, so when you drop your notes all over the floor you can put them back into order!

BACKGROUND PRINTING

You can continue to work in a file while it's printing by turning on Background Print. To check, or do this:

❶ Open the **Tools** menu and select options

❷ Select **Print tab**

❸ Select or clear **Background Printing**

SUMMARY

In this chapter we have covered the following:

✓ The different methods of printing slides.

✓ The different print set-up options.

5 | FORMATTING SLIDES

AIMS OF THIS CHAPTER

In this chapter we will be looking at the formatting tools in PowerPoint, and getting to grips with them. We will also be looking at the page setup and how to best use this to our advantage. By furthering our understanding of Master Slides, we will be learning how to create styles and backgrounds for our slides.

5.1 Page setup

Design templates, Presentation templates or AutoContent Wizard will all do a decent job, but to put your own mark on a presentation, it is important to understand basic formatting and page setup commands.

Page set up determines the basic shape and format of your slide, handout or notes by setting the size and orientation – *portrait* or *landscape*.

The **Page Setup** dialog box requires information about the medium upon which your presentation will be shown, e.g. transparencies, projector, paper (as handouts) and so forth, which determines the size of slides. The **Orientation** is also set here, and note that there are separate settings for *Slides* and for *Notes, handouts and outline*.

If you are creating your own styles for your presentation you will need to configure page setup before you start to put text and graphics onto the slides. There is nothing worse than working through the slides and then realizing the page hasn't been set up to meet the needs of the presentation!

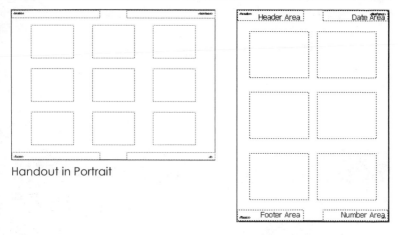

Handout in Portrait

Handout in Landscape

Figure 5.1 Two of the alternative Handout layouts, showing the use of different orientations

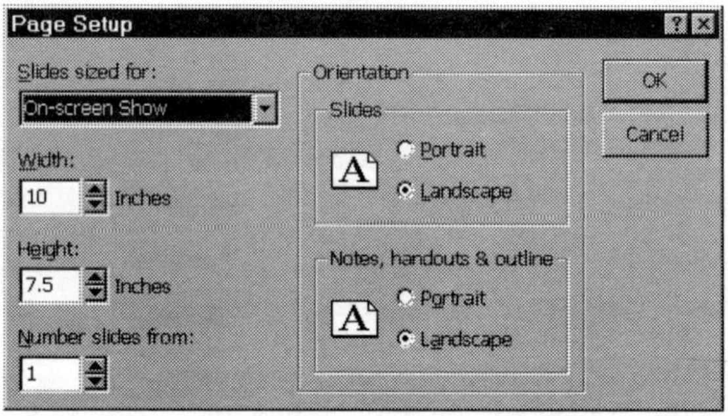

Figure 5.2 The **Page Setup** dialog box. **Width** and **Height** are set automatically by the **Slides sized for:** choice. A *Custom* option is available if required. Note the **Number slides from:** box. This can be useful if you are developing a large presentation in several sections and want to continue the slide numbering sequence across them all

5.2 Masters

If you are creating a presentation of
more than one slide, you can ensure
their consistency by using one of the
Master facilities. These are Slide Master, Title Master, Notes Master and
Handout Master, and can be reached
through the View menu.

Slide Master

The Slide Master controls the text styles and colours, the formatting of
the slides and colour schemes. It provides the placeholders for those
elements that are to be consistent throughout the presentation, such as
headers and footers, dates, page numbering and you can insert your
own placeholder to add in a logo or slogan, etc. (see Chapters 6 and 7).

If, having set up the Slide Master and created your presentation you
want to change the appearance of one slide you simply follow the same
procedures but at the end of setting up the particular option, such as
colour scheme, select **Apply**, not **Apply to all**. This will ensure that
only the slide you have on the screen will be affected.

In presentations created from templates and wizards, the Slide Master
has already been set up. It can, however be changed through the Slide
Master command in the **View** menu as it can be for a blank slide that
you are designing yourself.

The Slide Master settings can be defined at the start and changed or
redefined at any stage throughout the presentation.

Title Master

The Title Master works along the same lines as Slide Master, in as
much as it can set the formatting and paragraph styles. It can be used
whenever required, both at the start of a new presentation and at the
start of new sections within one. It can only be used though, with the
Title slide found in the **New Slide** dialog box.

Note that when you change Slide Master it will change any existing settings in every slide in the presentation, including the title slide. To make permanent changes to the title slide, the Title Master should be changed *after* the Slide Master has been changed.

Handout and Notes Master

These offer the facility to set up those elements on the handouts and notes pages that will appear throughout. For instance, this might be a logo, the date or time, page numbering and so on. They can be set up exactly as Slide Master or Title Master.

5.3 Formatting

The formatting of the masters and individual slides follow the same processes, using the menus in PowerPoint. The **Format, Insert** and **View** menus contain the options used for formatting, and most of these options can also be found on the Formatting toolbar. The particular commands we shall be looking at here are:

- **Header and Footer** on the **View** menu
- **Slide Number** and **Date and Time** on the **Insert** menu
- most of the options on the **Format** menu.

Generally the formatting commands work in the same way as they do in other Microsoft applications, such as Word.

View – Header and Footer

These are the entries that appear above (header) and below (footer) the body of the slide. They might contain the date, slide number, reference, document title, etc.

Headers and footers can be set up on the Slide Master or onto the individual slides (see section 5.6).

Insert – Slide Number

Use this when you want to display the number on selected individual slides, inserting it into an existing placeholder. To number a whole series of slides, the header and footer option should be used.

Insert – Date and Time

As with the Slide Number, use this if the display is only required on individual slides. The Date and Time can also be added through the header and footer.

5.4 The Format menu

Font

Opens the **Font** dialog box (see Figure 5.3) where you can set the type, size, colour and other aspects of the typeface used for text. Some Font format options can also be set from tools on the Formatting toolbar.

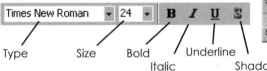

Type   Size   Bold   Underline
                Italic   Shadow

Bullets and Numbering

Opens the **Bullets and Numbering** dialog box (see Figure 5.4) where you can select the style of bullets or numbers used in lists. Paragraphs within bulleted lists can be demoted or promoted by clicking on the appropriate buttons on the formatting toolbar. Bullets and numbers can be set, in the default styles, from the toolbar buttons.

Numbered list   Bulleted list

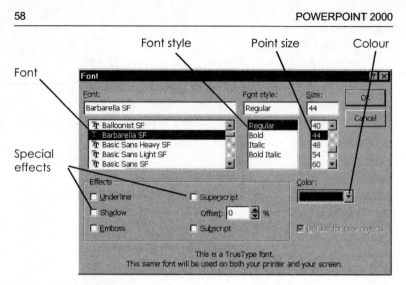

Figure 5.3 The **Font** dialog box. All aspects of fonts formatting can be set here

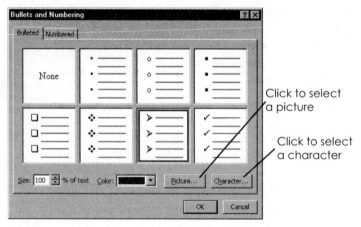

Figure 5.4 The **Bullets and Numbering** dialog box. You can use a ready made style, adjusting the **Size** or **Color** if required, or select a **Picture** (from the Clipart Gallery) or a **Character** (from the Character Map) to create your own bullet style

Alignment

- **Align left** sets the text blocked at the left margin and ragged at the right margin – each line starts at the same point on the left and when the text reaches the right margin it moves to the next line taking the next full word with it.

- **Center** will centre the line of text across the width of the text box, between its margins.

- **Align right** is the opposite of align left, lining the text up at the right side of the text box.

- **Justified** means the text and spaces are stretched or squeezed up across the page so that every line, except the last line of a paragraph, starts and ends at the same point.

The first three alignment options can also be set using the buttons on the Formatting toolbar.

Align left   /   Align right
Center

Line spacing

Enables you to change the line spacing from the default single line spacing, and to set the space between paragraphs.

The **Line spacing** can be set in *lines* or *points*. The number of points a line takes up depends on the font size within which you are working. For example, if you're using Times New Roman, size 12, the default line size will be 14. Increasing this to 18 will space out your text a little more. If the line size is less than the text size, the tops and bottoms of letters will start to disappear!

The **Before** and **After paragraphs** sets the space between paragraphs, again in either lines or points. For example, if you have text that must fit within a certain sized placeholder you could type it in, leave out line spaces between each paragraph and set up a space of 6 points before (or after) each paragraph.

Slide Layout

This provides the opportunity to change the layout of the slide to something different, e.g. from a 2-column text to one showing text and chart.

Slide Color Scheme

This opens the Color Scheme dialog box. Here you can select a new scheme or, on the Custom tab, adjust selected elements.

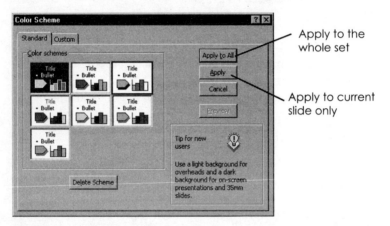

Apply to the whole set

Apply to current slide only

Figure 5.5 The **Color Scheme** dialog box. Select a ready-made scheme from the Standard tab, or go to the Custom tab to set the colours for background, text, shadows, etc. separately

Background

Allows you to set the appearance of the background of the current slide, or all slides, by changing its colour, pattern, shading or picture. Here, as in the Color Scheme dialog box, colours can be selected from the Colors palette. Use a **Standard** colour or define your own on the **Custom** tab.

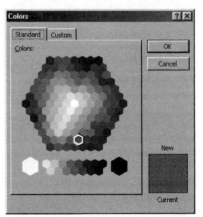

Apply Design Template

Use this if you've changed the default settings of a series of slides based on a template and want to revert to the original design.

Indented paragraphs

Paragraphs can be indented from the left and right margins by adjusting the *indent markers* on the ruler. Unlike Microsoft Word, there is no menu option for setting, or changing indents. However, by opening the ruler, found in the View menu, and moving the indent markers along it, you can set first line indents, left or right indents and hanging indents (see section 5.7).

5.4 Formatting individual slides

To format part of an individual slide you should select the placeholder and text within it and then open the appropriate menu. The following exercise gives practice in different types of formatting.

❶ Open a presentation that contains a bulleted list, or create a new one if necessary.

Start by formatting the title text so that it is much bolder and fills the placeholder, whilst making sure it doesn't go over on to two lines.

❶ Go to Slide 1.

❷ Select the Title placeholder.

❸ Highlight the Title text.

❹ Open the **Format** menu, and select **Font...**to open the **Font** dialog box (see Figure 5.3)

❺ From the list in the **Font** box select a suitable font.

To try out fonts, select the font you want and click the **Preview** button. This will apply the font to your slide – you may have to move the Font dialog box out of the way to be able to see it properly!.

❻ If necessary select a larger the **Font size**.

❼   Select any of the **Font styles** or **Effects** you feel would be
    appropriate, such as bold, italic, shadow or underline.

❽   Click **OK** to close the Font dialog box when you are happy
    with the formats.

Select other text items and apply formatting to them in the same way.

Don't use too many styles in one slide as it will start to look 'busy'. A
sensible guideline is to use no more than two fonts (with a range of
sizes) per presentation.

♦   Remember to keep clicking **Preview** to check how the
    changes are going.

Some formats can be applied by using the buttons on the Formatting
toolbar. The only difference is that you can't preview the settings.

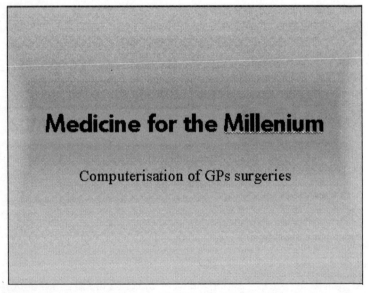

Figure 5.6 Slide 1 after formatting. The Title text has been defined
as Montreal SF, size 48 points, bold. Notice how the spell checker
has automatically picked up the mistype in *Millennium*, but has
failed to spot the missing apostrophe in *GPs'* – there is no substitute
for checking your own work carefully!

All you need to do is:

❶ Select the placeholder and highlight the text within it.

❷ Click on the drop-down arrow alongside the **Font** box and select a font – note that the fonts names are displayed in their own font.

❸ Click on the drop-down arrow alongside the **Font size** box and select the size.

❹ Click the buttons to make the text bold, italics, underlined or shadowed. Note that these are 'toggle switches'. Click again to turn the effect off.

❺ Now view the slides in Slide Show view to see how they look with the changes you've made.

Bullets and Numbering

❷ Go to the slide with the bulleted list placeholder and highlight the list.

❸ Open the **Format** menu.

❹ Select **Bullets and Numbering**.

❺ At the Bullets and Numbering dialog box (see Figure 5.4) change the bullet type from the current symbol to ❖. To do this, select the appropriate bullet style and click **OK**.

You can have several levels of bullets, or sub-lists within lists, each indented further from the left. To move a bullet item to a lower level is known as *demoting*.

❶ Place the insertion point after an item which could take some subsidiary points and press **[Enter]**.

❷ Click the **Demote** button on the toolbar once – the bullet will move to the right.

❸ Change the bullet point to something different, using the instructions above, to emphasis that this is a different level of indent.

❹ Enter some text and press **[Enter]** to create a new bullet point at the same level. (Notice how each time you press **[Enter]** the insertion point positions itself correctly with the bullet.)

◆ After entering the last item you will still have the indented line with the bullet. Press **[Enter]**, then **[Backspace]** until the bullet is deleted and the next line has moved up.

◆ Alternatively, if you want the line space but not the bullet, click on the **Bullet** button on the toolbar to deselect it.

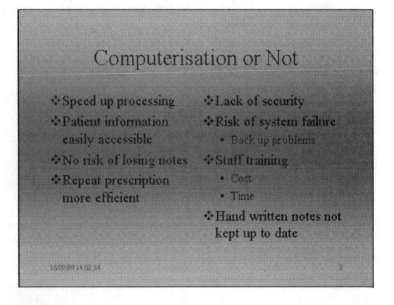

Figure 5.7 A bulleted list with two levels, each with its own bullet character

5.5 Formatting in Slide Master

The Slide Master holds the default settings for the format of title text, bullets and other common features. These settings can be overridden by applying formats to elements on individual slides. Changes made on the Slide Master will be applied to all the slides in the presentation, except where an element has already been formatted.

The previous practice task demonstrated how to use the formatting functions to change the look of individual slides. Now we need to look at integrating these same commands, and others to make changes to masters that will affect a whole series of slides or handouts.

❶ Close the presentation that is open on your computer and create a new one, selecting *Blank presentation*.

❷ Select a Title slide from the **New Slide** dialog box and click **OK**.

❸ Insert two more slides, *bulleted list* and *2-column text*.

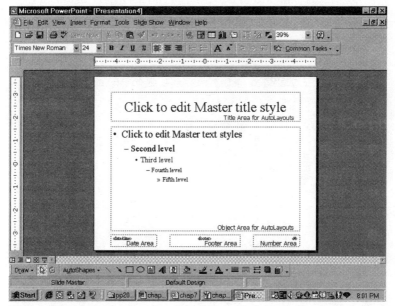

Figure 5.8 Slide Master, showing the initial default settings

Having created the slides needed for your presentation you can now format the Slide Master.

❶   Open the **View** menu.

❷   Point to **Master** and select **Slide Master**.

◆   It doesn't matter which slide you have on the screen, or which view you're in when selecting Slide Master, you will always be given a slide that will cover all variations of formatting, i.e. title text, bulleted lists, headers and footers and blank background.

The first thing to do when creating a Slide Master is plan the colour scheme for the slides. For this exercise, we'll create our own customized scheme.

To customize a colour scheme:

❶   Open the **Format** menu.

❷   Select **Slide Color Scheme**, and click on the **Custom** tab.

❸   In the **Scheme Colors** area, select **Background**.

❹   Click **Change Color**.

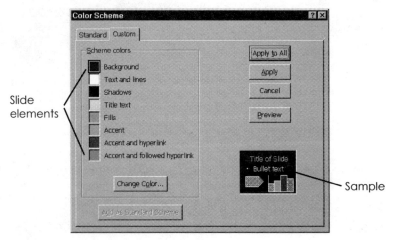

Figure 5.9 Setting a Custom Color Scheme

- ♦ You can double-click on a colour to go straight to the **Change Color...** panel.

- ❺ Select a colour, e.g. a pale blue, and click **OK**.

- ❻ Select **Text and lines** and change its colour in the same way. Repeat for each element in the list.

- ❼ On completion, if you're happy with the results of the sample, click on **Apply to All**.

- ❽ Save the presentation so that you don't lose the changes you have made!

Having established the colour scheme you can now adjust the background to the slide to make it more interesting than the currently selected, flat, solid colour.

- ♦ Open the **Format** menu and select **Background...**

The dialog box shows your existing colour scheme with the background colour in a box below it.

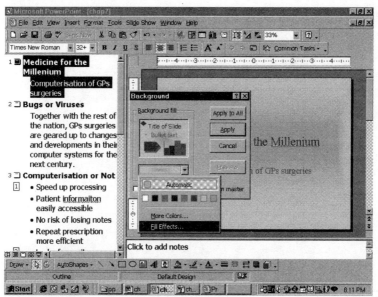

Figure 5.10 Setting the background to a slide

To change the background from being a flat solid colour simply click on the drop-down arrow alongside the background colour to see the range of options. As with colour scheme, you can change the background colour by either selecting one of the colours shown or clicking on **More colors...** and selecting from there.

The other choice is **Fill Effects...** which gives you great scope for making the background more interesting.

The options are arranged on four tabs: **Gradient, Texture, Pattern** and **Picture**. To use any of the effects, click on the tab to bring it to the front, select your choice and click **OK**.

♦   **Gradient** allows one or two colours with the gradient of colour going at various angles. The *Preset* choice offers a range of backgrounds already set up.

♦   **Texture** has a range of textured backgrounds to choose from. Note that when choosing texture the colour you've selected for the background previously will be replaced.

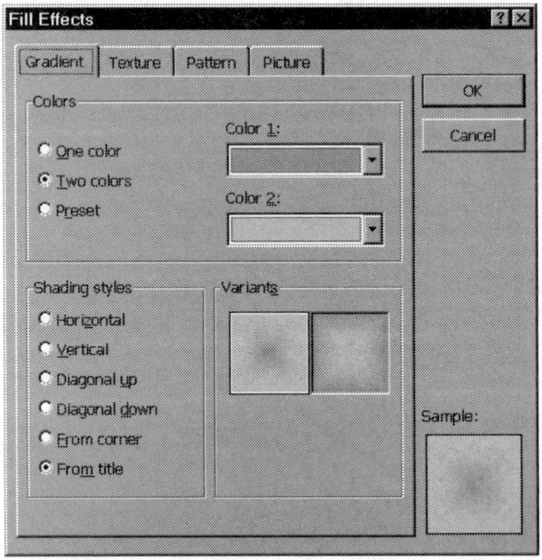

Figure 5.11 A custom-made two colour gradient can give you just the effect you want, but some of the Presets are very neat!

+ **Pattern** retains your selected background colour and selects a complementary colour to work with the original and so create a range of patterns. Both background and foreground colours can be changed.

+ **Picture** provides the facility to add a picture as the background. Click the **Select picture** button and select the folder or drive in which your pictures are stored, e.g. *CD drive*, *clipart folder*. Select the picture, and it appears in the Fill Effects dialog box, click **OK**.

For the **Slide Master** in this particular task you need to change the background so that it has a gradient effect:

❶ Open the **Format** menu and select **Background...**

❷ At the Background dialog box, click the drop-down arrow by the colour box and select **Fill Effects...**

❸ On the **Gradient** tab, select *Two colors*.

❹ Click the **Color 1** drop-down arrow and chose a colour. Repeat for **Color 2**.

❺ Select a **Shading style**, e.g. *From title*.

❻ On completion click on **OK**, and then **Apply to All**.

Fonts and bullets

Changing the fonts and bullets in Slide Master is exactly as demonstrated previously in formatting an individual slide.

5.6 Headers and footers

Headers and footers are used to hold information, such as date and time, slide or page number, author, etc. that you want to appear on every slide or page. Slides can only have footers; notes and handouts can have both headers and footers.

If these are set in Slide Master view, then they are applied to all slides. If set in any other view, they can be applied to the current slide or to all slides as required. Settings for notes and handouts apply to all pages, now matter which view you start in.

In this practice task you are working with Slide Master, but the same principles apply to setting headers and footers on the Notes and Handout masters.

❶ Open the **View** menu and select **Header and Footer...** to open the dialog box.

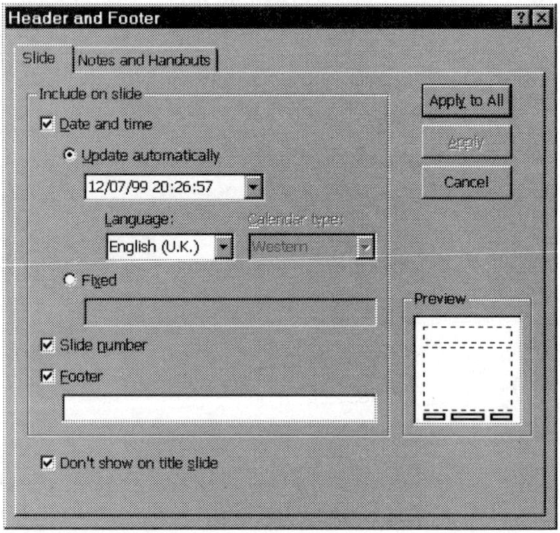

Figure 5.12 The **Slide** tab only has options for a footer. The **Notes and Handout** tab, has settings for headers and footers.

❷ Tick the **Date and time** checkbox to display this.

◆ Select **Update automatically**, if you want the current date to be displayed whenever the presentation is shown. Choose the date format from the drop down list.

◆ Select **Fixed**, and type in a date if you want to show when the slide was created or updated.

❸   If you wish to show slide numbers (these will be consecu-
     tive from 1 onwards) tick **Slide number**.

❹   If you want to add information into the footer, such as a
     file name make sure **Footer** has a tick beside it, then click
     into the box and type in the appropriate data.

❺   The information will appear on all slides unless you tick
     the **Don't show on title slide** option.

❻   On completion click on **Apply to all**. (Whilst in Slide
     Master view you will not see the results of these actions.)

❼   Now revert to Normal view and see how the settings in
     Slide Master have affected each slide in the presentation.

5.7 Indents

Text can be moved in from the left edge of its placeholder by setting
indents. To see this, let's add some text to our new slides.

❶   Return to the first slide and key in following title into the
     title placeholder:

     Medicine for the Millennium

❷   And in the subtitle placeholder insert:

     Computerization of GPs Surgeries

❸   Now move to Slide 2 and key in the following short para-
     graph into the text placeholder:

     **Together with the rest of the nation, GPs' surgeries are
     geared up to changes and developments in their
     computer systems for the next century.**

The text has a bullet point at the left of it (this is a bulleted list slide),
and as we're not going to insert anything else into that placeholder it
would be useful to get rid of this and remove the indent so that the text
starts at the left edge of the placeholder.

To adjust indents you need to see the **ruler** and indent markers. Slide
view is best for working with the ruler, though it can also be used in
Normal or Outline view.

Indents are displayed on the **ruler** by two triangular markers and a tiny block. The upper triangle adjusts the indentation of the first line of a paragraph; the lower triangle the indentation of the rest of a paragraph.

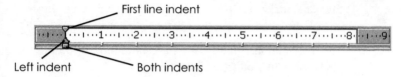

If the whole of a paragraph is to be indented then you should drag the rectangle below the left indent marker to the right along the ruler.

❶ Switch to Slide view and bring the ruler up onto the screen by selecting **Ruler** in the **View** menu.

♦ You need to remove the bullet and bring the body of the paragraph back to the left edge of the ruler.

❷ Position the insertion point at the start of the text.

❸ Click on the **Bullet** button on the toolbar to deselect it.

❹ Point to the **left indent marker**.

❺ Drag it to the left until it is directly below the **first line indent marker**.

❻ Release the mouse.

Completing the exercise

❶ In the title placeholder of Slide 2, key in the title:
    Bugs or Viruses

❷ Move to the third slide and key in the following title:
    Computerization or Not

❸ In the first column enter the following points:
    • Speed up processing
    • Patient information easily accessible
    • No risk of losing notes
    • Repeat prescription more efficient"

❹   In the second column add the following –use the **Demote**
      and **Promote** buttons on the toolbar for the second line
      indents:

      •   **Lack of security**
      •   **Risk of system failure**
      •   **Back-up problems**
            ◆   **Staff training**
            ◆   **Cost**
            ◆   **Time**
      •   **Hand written notes not kept up to date"**

❺   Save the presentation.

Individual slide variations

For some of the slides in your presentation it will not be necessary to
follow the set up of the Slide Master. You might have one slide that
doesn't need your corporate logo, or requires a different footer on it.
You might want it to have a different colour scheme. It is quite possible to do this. Until the last stage of most of the formatting processes
you follow the same procedures, but at the end select **Apply** not **Apply
to all**!

There is one final thing to do to this presentation, that is to change the
background of the third slide so that it is different from the others.
We'll retain the same colour schemes but modify it slightly.

❶   Return to the slide to be changed, i.e. Slide 3.

❷   From the **Format** menu select **Background.**

❸   Following the instructions given in section 5.5, change the
      background of this slide to something completely different,
      for instance a **Pattern**.

❹   On completion click **Apply**.

By clicking on **Apply** and not **Apply to all** the change will only take
effect on this slide.

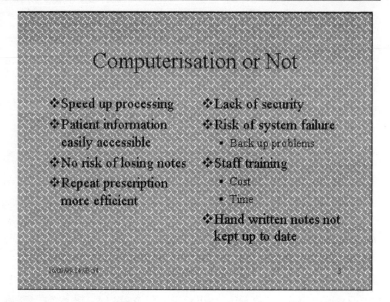

Figure 5.13 Slide 3 after a pattern background has been added

SUMMARY

In this chapter we have looked into:

✓ Formatting text and slides.

✓ Setting up Slide Masters.

✓ Adding headers and footers.

✓ Using indents.

6 | **CLIP ART AND WORDART**

AIMS OF THIS CHAPTER

In this chapter we will be looking at clip art and other types of images, as well as WordArt. By gaining basic knowledge of these tools we will be able to apply them to our slides.

6.1 Working with clip art

So far in this book we've concentrated on using predesigned facilities and text only in slides. Naturally there is a need for images, logos, charts or imported data (see Chapter 8 for these later points).

In this chapter we are going to look at the integration of *objects*, specifically clip art, pictures from other sources and WordArt.

Clip art is provided with the software installed on your computer or can be bought on CDs from computer retail outlets. There is a huge range of clip art available these days covering every conceivable subject or interest. An alternative source of clip art is the Internet. A picture can be copied directly into your PowerPoint file from the Internet or saved onto your hard drive for later use.

When using clip art from any source you should be aware of the copyright regulations put upon its use. For instance the images are probably not available for commercial use. If necessary you will have to gain permission to use the image from the person or organisation that owns the copyright.

Clip art can be inserted into a side from the New Slide selection containing a Clip art placeholder, or into any other position in a slide.

Clip art is selected from the Clip Gallery, a collection of images supplied with PowerPoint and other Microsoft Office software. The images are divided into categories such as Favorites (images you use regularly and choose to move to this location), Animals, Travel and so on.

Through the Clip Gallery you can download clip art from Microsoft's Web site and it will be added to your gallery.

Inserting clip art is very straightforward. Here's how:

◆   Create a new slide, selecting the *Clip Art and text* slide at the New Slide dialog box.

You now need to insert some clip art into the clip art placeholder. We're going to work with Clip Gallery rather than anything else.

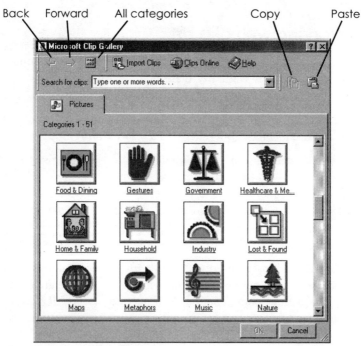

Figure 6.1 The Clip Gallery

• Select the clip art placeholder and double-click on the clip art icon  – this will take you into the Clip Gallery.

You can either browse through the categories to find an image, or enter a key word into the **Search for clip** box.

❶ When searching through the **Search for clips** box, type in a key word, e.g. *child*.

❷ Press **[Enter]** on the keyboard.

❸ The selection of images resulting from your search will appear on the screen.

❹ Scroll through the group on the screen, when you reach the end click ⌊🔡 to view the next group.
Keep Looking

Forward   List all categories

Back

Figure 6.2 The Clip Gallery after a search for 'child'

- To browse by category, scroll through the choice at the first screen and select the category you're interested in, e.g. *home and family*. Scroll through and find the image you want, clicking the **Keep looking** button if needed.

- Using either method you can retrace your steps by clicking on the **Back** button on the Clip Gallery toolbar.

❺ When you find a suitable image, click on it to select it.

Another menu will appear offering you the choice of inserting, previewing the clip (this is a toggle key – you can click on it and off to preview and close again), add the clip to your 'Favorites' category or find another similar clip.

- Insert the chosen clip into your slide by clicking on the top button in the menu.

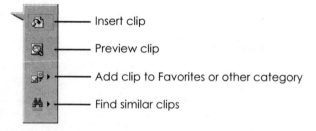

6.2 Inserting pictures

When creating your presentations it is not necessary to work only with clip art images. You can add a more personal, or corporate image to your work by importing photographs and scanned images. With a digital camera photographs can be taken and downloaded directly to your computer. Scanned images are acquired by putting your picture on to the scanner bed and scanning it into the computer. This type of image can be imported directly from the relevant piece of hardware into the presentation file or can be saved in an appropriate piece of software and then copied and pasted into a presentation file when required.

Images can also be inserted using the **Picture** option on the **Insert** menu. From here select **Clip Art...** for the Clip Gallery, or select images from an alternative source. For instance to insert a picture from a

CD, open the **Insert** menu, select **Picture**, then **From File...** You can then browse your folders to locate and select your picture.

To insert a scanned image select the **From Scanner or Camera...** option, then follow the usual steps, for your computer, to scan an image. Having finished scanning, the image will automatically be inserted into your PowerPoint file.

When scanning in pictures or photographs just bear in mind that they take up a large amount of hard disk space and will consequently slow down the presentation. You should, therefore, use them sparingly.

Resolution and file formats

When working with scanned images or digital photographs you need to consider *resolution*. This is the number of dots per inch (dpi) of the picture. The resolution that is used to download the image is not as important as the resolution capabilities of the output device, for instance the printer. If your printer has resolution of 300 dpi then the original image should be at least 300 dpi. When importing your picture it might be worth reducing it to about 60% of its actual size. This will compact the dpi into a smaller area, therefore giving a sharper image.

The file format of picture or clip art files will differ depending on the software used to create them. Graphics files, for example, created in Windows' Paint software use the Bitmap format (BMP). Internet pictures are quite often stored with a JPEG format (JPEG). This, together with others such as TIF (Tagged Image File Format) and GIF (Graphics Image File Format) can be opened into most computer systems and software. It is worth bearing in mind that TIFs retain more accurate data of a scanned image.

If you have image files in a format that PowerPoint cannot handle, you can convert them into a suitable format with graphics software such as Paint Shop Pro (available through the Internet at http://www.jasc.com).

Sizes of clip art, photographs and scanned images vary considerably but can be huge. It is probably better, therefore, to keep 'thumbnails' of these files on your computer instead of the actual file so that minimal space is taken up by them. A thumbnail is a miniature view of a picture which can be previewed for selection purposes, as in the Microsoft Clipart Gallery.

6.3 The Picture toolbar

Having inserted any type of picture, images from a CD or a scanned image the Picture toolbar will open on your screen – if it does not open, right-click on any toolbar and select **Picture** from the shortcut menu.

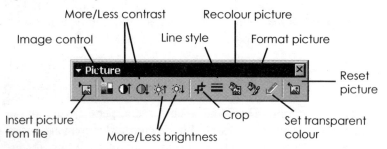

This can be used for formatting the picture. Working from left to right, the tools are:

- ♦ **Insert picture from file** opens the Insert Picture dialog box.

- ♦ **Image control** lets you change the picture from its automatic colours to black and white, greyscale or watermark – a pale, low contrast image, that can make an effective background.

- ♦ The **Contrast** and **Brightness buttons** work with coloured, greyscale and black and white pictures. Use them lightly to improve the colour or contrast balance of photographs or clip art, or heavily for special effects – bleaching out light colours, or deepening shadows.

- ♦ The **crop tool** enables you to trim the picture.

♦   **Line style** changes the type of line around the picture.

♦   **Recolour picture** can only be used on clip art drawings.
    It allows you to replace any of the original colours with
    new ones from the selection or from the full palette.

Recolouring clip art

❶   Select the clip art picture.

❷   Click the Recolour picture button.

❸   Click on an **original** colour.

❹   In the **new** colour list, click the drop-down arrow.

❺   Select **More colors...**

❻   Choose a new colour, and click **OK**.

As you select
colours from
More Colors...
they are
added to the
initial set

♦   **Set transparent colour** allows you to set one colour as
    transparent, so that the slide background shows through.
    This can only be used on photographs, scanned or other
    images in JPG, GIF or BMP format.

♦   **Reset picture** will reset any changes made back to the
    original settings.

Using the clip art image, experiment with the other buttons to see what
effects you can achieve.

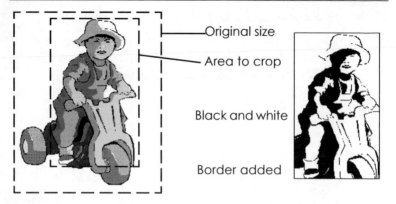

Original size

Area to crop

Black and white

Border added

Figure 6.4 Showing the use of some of the tools. The picture has been cropped to focus on the child, then set to pure black and white, using the Image Control option, and made darker. To finish it off, the Line tool was used to add a border.

6.4 Using WordArt

WordArt provides a range of layouts and styles for text. It might be used to provide headings and titles that will catch the viewer's eye. These can stand out more and be more striking than text that has simply been formatted using the font types and styles discussed earlier.

When using WordArt, you don't need to select an existing placeholder, as it creates its own on selection.

There are three ways of starting WordArt:

♦   Click the **WordArt** [4] button on the Drawing toolbar.

♦   Open the **Insert** menu, point to **Picture** and select **WordArt**.

♦   Open the **Insert** menu, point to **Object** and select *Microsoft WordArt* from the **Insert Object** dialog box.

The first two enable you to work with it in the same way, the third is slightly different. Here we will concentrate on using the first method and very briefly touch on the third.

❶   Click the **WordArt** ◢ button.

❷   The **WordArt gallery** opens. Select a style and click **OK**.

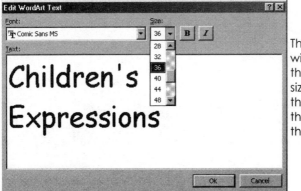

Figure 6.4 The WordArt Gallery

❹   Type in your text.

❺   Select the font and the size you want.

❻   Click **OK**.

The Edit window shows the font and size, but not the layout of the text. Keep the sizes large!

The WordArt placeholder will appear on the slide (probably in the centre). It can be moved by dragging on the frame, and resized by dragging handles in and out.

❶ Reposition the **placeholder** so that it comes at the top of the slide, in the centre.

❷ **Resize** it so that it fills the width of the slide.

You will see that the WordArt placeholder has a little yellow diamond beside or underneath it. This is the adjustment handle, and its effect varies according to the gallery style in use. By dragging on it you can slant upright text, change the angle of diagonal text, or the curvature of an arc or the depth of a perspective view, or the wrap amount of a cylindrical layout. Play with it and watch what it does!

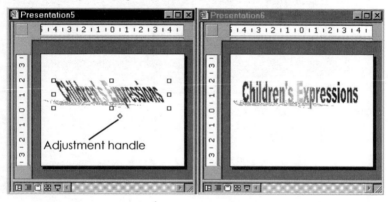

Figure 6.5 Adjusting the size and position of a WordArt object

The WordArt toolbar opens automatically when the WordArt object is selected.

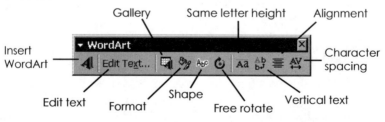

- **Insert WordArt** opens the gallery so that you can create a new WordArt object.

- **Edit text** enables the font type, size and style to be changed.

- **Gallery** allows you to choose a new style for the existing object.

- **Format** opens the Format WordArt dialog box which gives you more control over the colours, fill patterns and outline of the text, its size, scale and position on the slide. You have the same choice of colours, fill patterns and textures here as for the background (see section 5.5).

- **Shape** opens a palette of shapes, and there is more variety here than in the main Gallery. The ring effects can be very striking – though they can make the text hard to read!

- The **Rotate** button places green rotation handles onto the placeholder. Position the pointer directly over one of these and the placeholder will rotate as you drag the mouse one way or the other.

- **Same letter height** will make all the letters equal size, whether they're lower case or upper case, or mixed.

- **Vertical text** will turn it round so that it goes vertically downwards.

- **Alignment** will align or stretch text within the placeholder.

- **Character spacing** will enable adjustment of spacing between letters.

All of these tools can be manipulated to adjust the appearance of your text until you achieve the desired result.

- Use the tools from the toolbar to change the font so that it's as near to a child's handwriting as possible, pink and in a wavy line.

As mentioned previously, WordArt can be accessed through the Object option of the Insert menu. When started this way, the WordArt application is opened within PowerPoint, with its own toolbar and menus. You aren't offered the range of predesigned styles, but you do have the facilities to create your own.

Figure 6.6 The finished WordArt object

SUMMARY

This chapter covered the following:

✓ Locating and inserting clip art.

✓ Adjusting pictures.

✓ Inserting and formatting WordArt.

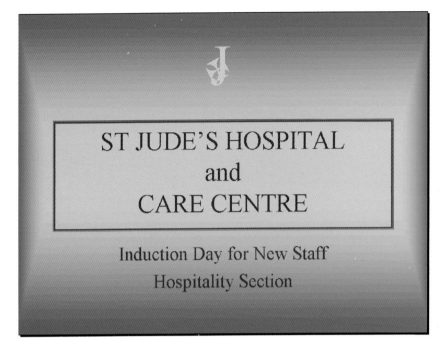

Plate 1 Opening slide for practice project 1

Plate 2 Slide with inserted image file (practice project 1)

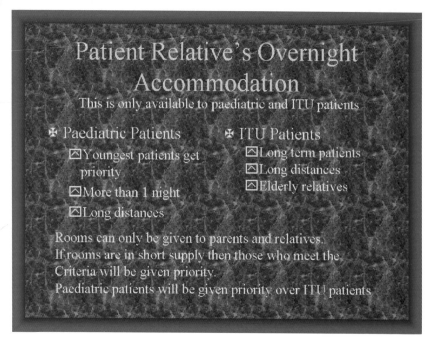

Plates 3–6 Different treatments of the same material

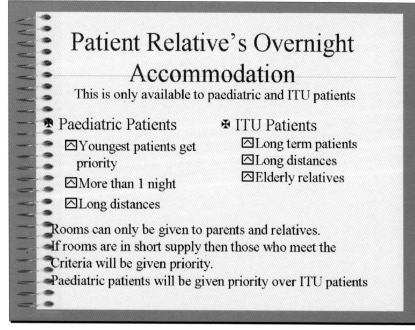

Plate 4

Patient Relative's Overnight Accommodation

This is only available to paediatric and ITU patients

✠ Paediatric Patients
- Youngest patients get priority
- More than 1 night
- Long distances

✠ ITU Patients
- Long term patients
- Long distances
- Elderly relatives

Rooms can only be given to parents and relatives.
If rooms are in short supply then those who meet the
Criteria will be given priority.
Paediatric patients will be given priority over ITU patients

Plate 5

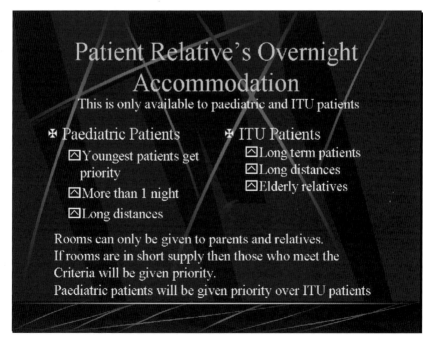

Plate 6

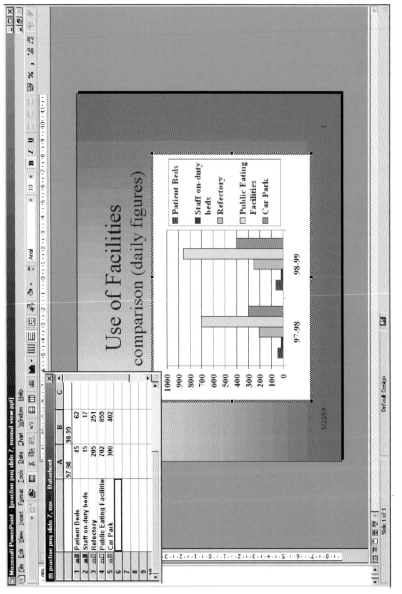

Plate 7 Graph 2000 being used to create a chart

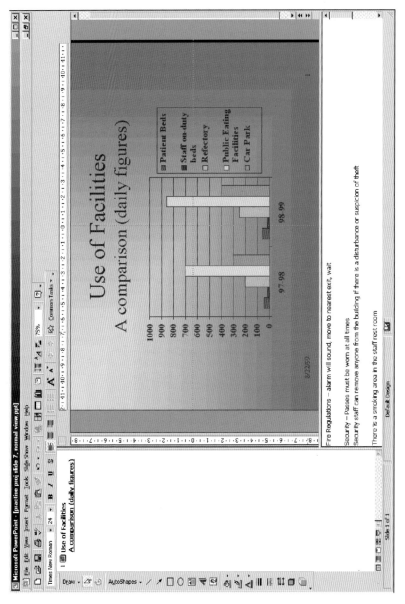

Plate 8 Slide with Graph 2000 chart and notes, seen here in Normal view

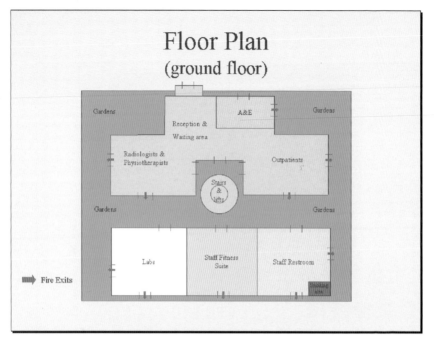

Plate 9 Diagram constructed with Drawing tools

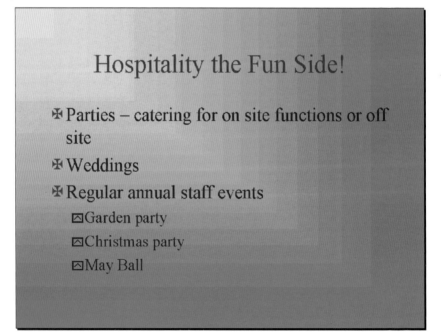

Plate 10 Customized bullets used to enliven lists

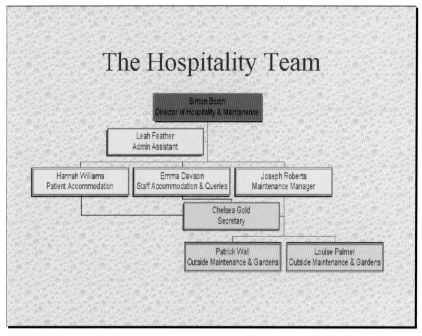

Plate 11 Slide with Organization Chart

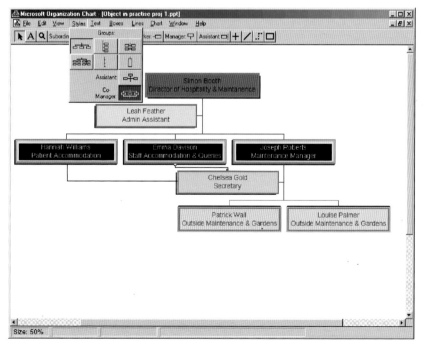

Plate 12 The chart under construction

Plate 13 Slide with hyperlink to main site

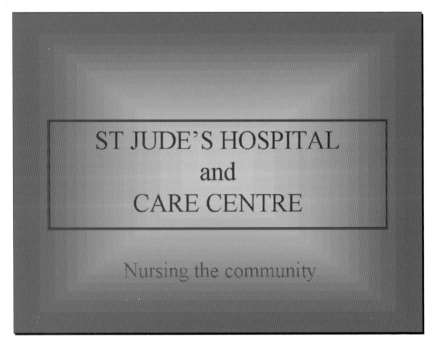

Plate 14 Closing slide for practice project 1

7 | DRAWING OBJECTS

AIMS OF THIS CHAPTER

In this chapter we will be looking into creating and manipulating images using the Drawing toolbar.

7.1 The Drawing toolbar

The tools on the Drawing toolbar serve two main purposes, to create new images and to manipulate the colour schemes and formatting of other objects, such as clip art pictures.

It contains the tools for inserting text, WordArt and Clip art, for drawing basic shapes, lines and arrows, and for setting the colour schemes for text and objects. It also contains the **AutoShape** menu offering options of different shapes and tools, together with the **Draw** menu offering tools for manipulating and formatting objects.

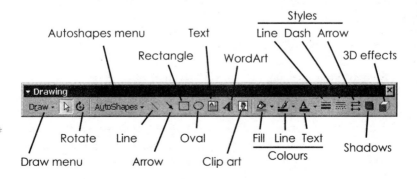

7.2 Simple lines and shapes

The Drawing toolbar contains two basic shape tools, **Rectangle** and **Oval** together with a **Line** tool and an **Arrow** tool.

The Rectangle and Oval can be selected and drawn on the slide by positioning the mouse pointer and dragging it to create the size of rectangle or oval needed. By holding down **[Shift]** while dragging the mouse, a square or circle will be formed.

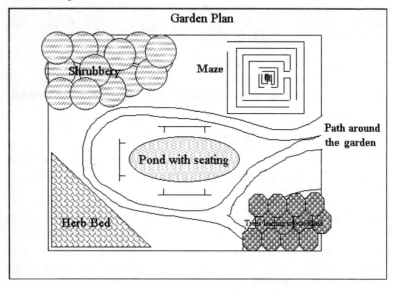

Figure 7.1 Using the lines and shapes to create a diagram

7.3 AutoShapes

The **AutoShapes** menu contains a selection of categories including Lines, Connectors, Basic Shapes, Flowchart elements, Stars and Banners, Callouts (thought bubbles) and Action Buttons (see Chapter 10). Each category contains a number of different shapes. By selecting one, positioning the mouse pointer on the slide and dragging it across, the shape will appear and be set at the size you choose.

Many of the AutoShapes have an adjustment handle which if dragged one way or another enables you to change the appearance of the shape. Experiment with this on different Autoshapes to see the results.

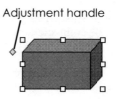

Adjustment handle

All the shapes, whether they are created from the toolbar shape buttons or the AutoShape menu can be resized, rotated, flipped and coloured and manipulated like any other placeholder. Text can be added to a shape, which then becomes part of the shape so that whatever you do will affect both the shape and text.

♦   If you want a shape that is a predefined size then select it from the toolbar or **AutoShape** menu, click once onto the slide and the shape will be inserted.

Also available within **AutoShapes** are straight lines, single-headed and double-headed arrows, curved lines, freeform lines and scribble.

By selecting **scribble** a pencil will appear with which you can draw freehand. The final object will be surrounded by a single placeholder.

Straight lines and the **arrow** choices are exactly as they seem, straight lines and arrows!

Curved and **freeform** lines enable you to draw lines with bends or angles in them by clicking the mouse at the point where the angle or curve should be and then double-clicking to end. On completion, the lines will be surrounded by one placeholder and can be moved and manipulated as one object, although they cannot be ungrouped.

The other AutoShape option available is **Connectors**. These lines are designed to connect objects together. They will move with the connected objects and have an adjustment handle which can be dragged to change the shape of the line. By moving the end of a connector it will detach itself from the object and can be locked to another point on the same or a different object. To remove a connector from two objects, drag the line in the middle and it will come away from both. If connected objects are moved, their connectors might need to be rerouted.

Create a new blank slide. We're going to add in some shapes which will be connected together with each one depicting a particular aspect of healthy living, as shown in Figure 7.2.

❶   Select a shape, e.g. *octagon* from the **Basic shapes** in **AutoShapes** and place it in the top left of the slide.

❷   Select another two shapes, a *cross*, from **Basic shapes** and a *5-point start* from **Stars and banners** and position them on the slide.

❸   Select a *heart* as the fourth shape, from **Basic shapes** and place this in the bottom right hand corner of the slide.

❹   Select each shape in turn and type in the following:

Exercise	Diet
Long Life	Good Health

By selecting a shape and an option from the Drawing toolbar you can make any number of changes to their appearance, for instance using the **3D effects** or **Shadows.**

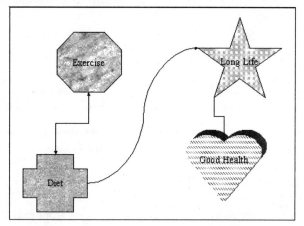

Figure 7.2 Image created from four basic shapes, joined by connectors. The shapes' fill and line colours, line thickness and styles can be set through the buttons on the Drawing toolbar

Connectors

These shapes are all going to be joined together with **connectors**.

❶ Open **Connectors** from the **Auto-Shapes** menu.

❷ Select a connector that can join the first shape to the second, ensuring that it has an arrow pointing to the second shape.

❸ Move the mouse over the first shape – notice how blue handles appear on the shape.

❹ Position the mouse pointer over one of these blue handles.

❺ Drag the mouse over to the second shape, and click on the blue handle that you want to connect to. If you use an Elbow or Curved connector, the line will take a path that does not go across either shape.

❻ Repeat these steps to join each shape to the next.

Usually, if you move one or more of the objects that are joined together the connectors will reroute automatically whilst still attached to the objects. If for some reason this doesn't happen, select the object, open the **Draw** menu and select **Reroute connectors**. All the connectors attached to that object will be redrawn so that they take new paths that do not go across any other objects. If you only want to reroute a single connector, select it before using the Reroute command.

CAN YOU SEE WHAT YOU'RE DOING?

If you want to view the detail on your slide more clearly, click the drop-down arrow in the **Zoom** box on the Standard toolbar and change the view to 100% (or greater).

7.4 Manipulating and formatting objects

The Drawing tools enable you to add aspects to your slide to make individual items stand out and enhance their appearance. You can also use them to assist with the formatting of elements in your slides, realign them in relation to other objects, turn or flip them.

Draw menu commands

Order enables you to changes the order of overlapping objects. Move them one layer at a time with **Send Backward** or **Bring Forward**, or through the stack with **Send to Back** and **Bring to Front**.

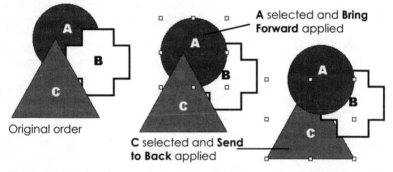

Original order

A selected and **Bring Forward** applied

C selected and **Send to Back** applied

Nudge moves a selected object 2 mm **Up**, **Down**, **Left** or **Right**. This is only for dedicated mouse users as you can move objects quicker, easier and more accurately with the keyboard.

❶   Select an object.

❷   Press an arrow key to move the object 2 mm in the direction of the arrow until it is in roughly the right place.

❸   Hold down **[Control]** and use the arrow keys for the final accurate positioning.

◆   **Rotate or flip** – does just that! **Free rotate** turns the object round in the direction you select (see Chapter 6). **Flip** will flip the object vertically or horizontally.

Change AutoShape enables you to choose a new AutoShape for a selected AutoShape object.

The **Edit points** command is for use with Freeform objects. If you select an object then use **Edit points** from the **Draw** menu, you can adjust its shape by dragging the points (handles) in or out.

All of these tools can be used to manipulate and format individual objects or groups of objects on the slide.

Selecting multiple elements

If you decide that a number of elements will be filled with the same colour or effect, or have the same outline, it is not necessary to change each element individually.

Select the first, hold down **[Shift]** and click on the next, to select it. Keep **[Shift]** down until you have clicked on all the elements you need.

You can select all the elements at once by pointing the cursor just above the top left corner of the image and dragging it diagonally down to the bottom right corner. All the elements within the box will be selected.

Format menu commands

The **Format** menu has an option for **Text box**, **AutoShape** or **Picture**, depending on the object you have selected. This opens a dialog box where you can perform such tasks as resizing, repositioning, changing the colour schemes, cropping a picture, or adjusting an object in relation to the text included within it.

    ◆   The dialog box can also be accessed by right-clicking on an object and selecting **Format ...** from the shortcut menu.

Return to the slide containing the AutoShape objects (see Figure 7.2). If necessary use the **Reroute** option in the **Draw** menu to move the connectors so that they're still attached to all the shapes. It looks as though two of them, the 5-point star and heart, are not quite big enough for their text. We can adjust this in the Format Autoshape dialog box:

    ❶   Select the 5-point star.

    ❷   Open the **Format** menu and select **AutoShape**.

    ❸   Click on the **Text box** tab.

Set the position of the text on the object

Text will go in one long line if this is off

Enlarge or shrink as needed

Rotate text clockwise

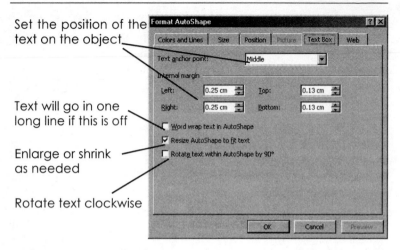

In this instance, all the settings are fine, except for the size of AutoShape in relation to the amount of text.

❶   Click a tick into **Resize AutoShape to fit text**.

❷   Click on **OK**. The star will increase in size just enough to contain the text.

❸   Repeat this for any of the other shapes that need it.

◆   If you **[Shift]** select the objects first, you can use the Format options on them all at once rather than individually.

You can use the dialog box for other purposes as well as text layout, for instance, to change the colours of the objects as well as changing the dimensions of an object and its position on the slide.

A simpler way of doing this, however, is to use the mouse and drag the object to move it and drag a handle on the object to resize it. By dragging whilst holding down **[Alt]** you will temporarily remove the **grid lines** from the slide and so have more flexibility in repositioning.

❶   Select the cross AutoShape on your slide.

❷   Point at the bottom right handle and drag the handle out so that the shape is twice the size – notice how the connectors move with the shape.

❸   Select the heart shape.

❹   Drag it into the centre of the slide.

❺   Resize the heart by dragging out the bottom right handle
     (the connector might need to be realigned to reattach to
     the heart).

7.5 Editing clip art objects

Although you can use the picture toolbar to reformat pictures (see Chapter 6), it doesn't provide the same flexibility as the Drawing toolbar. A clip art object is made up of a number of parts, which are all grouped together to create a picture. The picture can be *ungrouped* so that individual elements of it can be changed. For instance, a different colour scheme could be used for a hand, or outlines added to some parts and not others. You are also able, having ungrouped the image, to select more than one group, or even to *regroup* the whole picture.

The **Grouping** commands can be accessed from the shortcut menu through the right mouse button or from the **Draw** menu. The following exercise gives practice in ungrouping and grouping:

❶   Create a new Blank presentation. From the **New Slide**
     dialog box select the *Blank* option.

It is recommended that you work in Slide view for this, as it will probably be easier to have the full screen in which to view the slide.

❷   Click the **Clip art** icon on the Drawing toolbar, and insert
     an image from the Clip Gallery.

❸   Click on the **Draw** menu and select **Ungroup**. If you are
     prompted to convert it to a Drawing object, select **Yes**.

When the file has been ungrouped it will have dozens of handles all over it. Each pair of handles 'holds' one tiny element of the picture, it might be something as small as a hand or as large as the torso, if this is just one shape.

❶   Click away from the ungrouped picture to deselect all the
     elements and reveal the image again.

❷   Click on one section to select it.

❸   Select a different colour from the **Fill colour** button on
     the toolbar.

◆   Follow these steps to re-colour the whole image.

The drop-down menus alongside the colour buttons on the toolbar open
up a range of different colours and also colour effects or line effects
that can be used. Selecting the different colours and effects is the same
process as if you were selecting colours and effects for the slide colour
scheme, as discussed in Chapter 7.

Grouping

When you have finished adjusting the elements of the image, form
them back into one object for ease of handling.

❶   Click and drag over the area to select all objects.

❷   Open the **Draw** menu and select **Group**.

Though these examples of grouping and ungrouping have been with
clip art objects, the commands can be used with any drawn objects.
When you create an image out of lines, shapes and autoshapes, grouping the elements into one object will make the image easier to handle.

7.6 Text with Drawing tools

On any slide, blank or predesigned, you can insert text into a placeholder
selected from the Drawing toolbar.

❶   Locate the area of the slide that you want to write on.

❷   Click on the **Text** button 🔳 on the Drawing toolbar.

❸   Click the insertion point onto the slide where you want
     the text to be typed, e.g. top left corner.

❹   Type in some text.

Notice that as you type, the size of placeholder will increase to accommodate the text. It will also increase in size if the font is made larger.

Text is, by default, left aligned. To set a different alignment, click an Alignment button on the Formatting toolbar. As you type in the text, it and the insertion point will be aligned accordingly.

- ♦ Note that you can drag the side handles to increase the width of the text box, making it as wide as you like to accommodate text to be typed in later. Dragging the top and bottom handles has no effect. The height is fixed by the number of lines of text in the box.

To set the Alignment, you only need to select the text box. For most other aspects of text formatting, you must select the words by high-lighting them. You can remove the highlight but retain the selection of the placeholder by clicking on the white space within it. If you click outside the placeholder the highlight will be removed and the placeholder will be deselected.

The text can be formatted by using the options on the Formatting toolbar or menus. Its colour can be set through the Font option in the Format menu or through the Font colour button on the Drawing toolbar.

Shadows close behind letters can be adding by clicking the **Shadow** button ▨ on the Formatting toolbar.

Deeper shadows for the text – and any drawn items – can be added through the Drawing toolbar.

- ♦ Click the **Shadow** button ▨ and select a style from the palette.

Only a limited range of styles is available for text. The full range can only be used on shapes and images.

The outline colour and thickness, and the background colour or pat-tern, can be set for the text placeholder, using the buttons on the Draw-ing toolbar.

- ♦ When putting in a background colour you will lose any shadow effect that you might have included on the text. The shadow will still be visible, however, on the outline of the placeholder.

So, returning to your slide, you should now have one line of text inserted at the top. You will probably have noticed that you can't really see the text within the placeholder because it's so small.

❶ Highlight the text and increase its size to 24 points and the change the font style to Arial Rounded MT Bold.

❷ If the text now more than fills the width of the placeholder, it will wrap onto another line. If the line splits at a bad point, position the insertion point where you would like to start the second line and press **[Enter]**.

To centre the text across the width of the placeholder:

❶ Highlight the text and click the **Center** button on the Formatting toolbar.

❷ Adjust the size of the placeholder so that it stretches evenly across the width of the slide, by dragging the handle on the right side.

◆ Remember to make sure there is the same distance from the placeholder to the right edge of the slide as there is from the left edge of the slide to the placeholder. If necessary use the ruler to help.

With this same text placeholder you can now format the colours and style of the text and placeholder.

❶ Highlight the text and click on the **Font color** button on the Drawing toolbar.

❷ Click a colour from the selection, or from the **More Font Colors...** palette.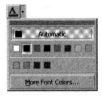

❸ Remove the highlight from the text.

❹ Click on the **Shadow** button on the Drawing toolbar and select *Shadow style 6.*

While the placeholder is selected the shadow will not be visible. Deselect the placeholder by clicking outside it and the shadow will become visible.

❶   Select the placeholder again and click the arrow on the **Fill color** button on the Drawing toolbar.

❷   Select **More Fill Colors...** and choose a colour.

❸   Click **Fill color** again, and select **Fill Effects...**

❹   Select **Gradient** and for **Shading style** choose *From corner*. Click **OK**.

Again the effect won't show until the placeholder has been deselected.

SUMMARY

We have covered the following in this chapter:

✓ Drawing objects using the tools on the Drawing toolbar.

✓ Adding AutoShapes and Connectors.

✓ Manipulating objects with the Draw menu commands.

✓ Adding text and formatting it through the Format Autoshapes dialog box.

8 | POWERPOINT AND OTHER APPLICATIONS

AIMS OF THIS CHAPTER

In this chapter we will be looking at how to use PowerPoint 2000 with other applications, in particular with Microsoft Graph and Organization Chart.

8.1 Opening files into PowerPoint

PowerPoint, like all the Office applications can be integrated with its partners in the suite. You are also able to insert files from other applications as long as PowerPoint can recognize the format.

The simplest way of importing information from another application is to open the file into PowerPoint. It will then be converted into a slide, or series of slides incorporating the data. For instance a Word file with a bulleted list of data could be opened into PowerPoint and be converted into a PowerPoint slide.

As a general rule, each paragraph will be converted into a new slide, i.e. one for the title, a second for the bulleted list, so you will need to do some reorganization. It will not necessarily put your text into the types of placeholders you would prefer.

❶ Open Word and create a new blank document. In it type the following title:

PowerPoint can use files saved in other formats

❷ Save the file and close it.

❸ Start PowerPoint and select **Open an existing presentation**, or or switch to it and use **File – Open**.

❹ In the **Open** dialog box, find the folder containing your file, for instance *My Documents*.

❺ You'll notice that the folder does not show your Word files, as the default is to list only PowerPoint presentations. Change the option in the **Files of Type** box to show all files by clicking the drop-down arrow and selecting *All files*. Your Word file will now appear in the list of files.

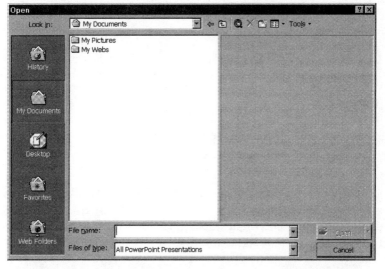

❻ Select the Word file and click **Open**. PowerPoint will convert the file and select a slide layout for the imported file.

❼ Save the PowerPoint file.

Your file will have been opened into PowerPoint but the title will probably have been inserted as the first item in a bulleted list! To move this to the title placeholder:

❶ Highlight the text, open the **Edit** menu, and select **Cut**.

❷ Click the insertion point into the title placeholder, open the **Edit** menu again and click **Paste**.

Files from any other Office application can be opened into PowerPoint in this way.

IMPORTING FROM OTHER SYSTEMS

You might be in a position where you need to insert files from another operating system. Usually PowerPoint will be able to convert the information into a format it can read, but always check through the **Files of type** box in the Open dialog box to view the list of formats and select the one that relates to your file. If there isn't one listed don't despair! Select *All files* and see if PowerPoint will list your file.

8.2 Moving between applications

One skill that is essential when trying to copy or cut between applications, or files is the ability to move between them quickly. It is not necessary to close down an application before opening a different one. You simply click its icon on the Windows Taskbar.

If you reach the point where you have so many application icons on the task bar that you can't see them all, then you can jump between them to find the one you want by holding down **[Alt]** and pressing **[Tab]**. An application and file name will flash up on the screen. Every time you press **[Tab]** the details of the next application will be seen. When you find the one you want, release the keys.

8.3 Copying/cutting and pasting

This is the most commonly used form of moving or copying data from one file or application to another, or within one file. It is also the most useful when inserting information into PowerPoint as you can stipulate the slide layout you want and exactly where the text or data should be inserted. You will find these tools on the Standard toolbar of every Windows application.

Cut   Copy   Paste

To copy or move something:

❶   Select the data.

❷   Open the **Edit** menu and select **Copy** or **Cut** (to move), or
     click the appropriate tools on the toolbar.

❸   Switch to the target file or application, if necessary, and
     position the insertion point where the data is to be inserted.

❹   Open the **Edit** menu and select **Paste** or click the **Paste**
     tool on the Standard toolbar.

If you are pasting into a different file or different application, it is perfectly safe to close the source file or application and open the other to
paste in the data. You can do this because the data is saved in an area of
memory called the Clipboard. This is standard on Windows systems
and will retain the data until you copy or cut something else. When
you turn the computer off anything in the Clipboard will be deleted.

❶   Return to the Word file you were working with previously.

❷   Insert the following paragraph of text:

     **Why create work for yourself by retyping text and data
     into PowerPoint when you've already got it as another file.
     Even though you might not want to insert the whole file
     you could copy and paste individual paragraphs.**

❸   Copy the text saved in the Word file using the **Edit – Copy**
     command or the **Copy** button.

❹   Switch to PowerPoint.

❺   Click the insertion point into the empty placeholder.

❻   Select **Paste** from the **Edit** menu or click the **Paste** button.

This same procedure can be used for copying/cutting and pasting between any application and PowerPoint or within files in PowerPoint.
For instance if you want to move the information around within slides
the simplest way of doing this is to use cut and paste.

Text or data pasted in this way is referred to as an *embedded object*.
This means that it has become part of the destination file.

8.4 Paste Link

The alternative method of copying information is to paste it as a *linked object*. In other words it will always retain a link to the original document it was copied from, the *source* file. Whenever that document is updated, the data pasted into the *destination* file will also be updated. If you want to create a linked object in the destination file you would copy and paste it using the **Paste Link** command.

❶   Return to the PowerPoint file you have been using in this chapter. Highlight the paragraph and press **[Delete]**.

❷   Return to the Word file from where the text was pasted and copy it again.

❸   Back in PowerPoint file, select the placeholder into which the text will be pasted.

❹   Open the **Edit** menu.

❺   Select **Paste Special** (if this doesn't appear straight away point onto the double arrow at the bottom of the menu).

❻   Select the *Paste Link* option, and click **OK**.

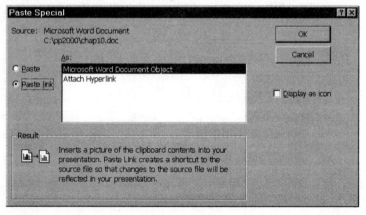

❼   Return again to the Word file and edit it.

❽   Return to the PowerPoint screen and check to see that the text in the slide has also changed.

These steps are particularly useful when pasting from Excel or Access as these are more likely to contain data that is frequently updated. For instance, if you use PowerPoint to do monthly presentations to a sales team, you can insert sections of a spreadsheet showing sales figures or forecasts, etc. Every month as that spreadsheet is updated then the slide in your presentation will also be updated, as long as you use Paste Link.

8.5 Graph 2000

It is perfectly possible to create a chart in Excel and paste or paste link it into a presentation, but charts can also be created very easily from within PowerPoint using Microsoft Graph 2000.

◆ Create a new presentation, selecting *Chart slide* at the New Slide dialog box. This slide has a title placeholder and chart placeholder, marked by the chart icon. Double-click on the icon to access the Graph window.

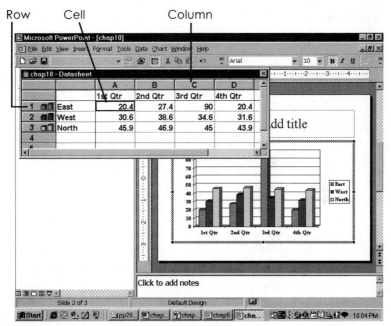

Figure 8.1 Graph 2000 when you start work on a new chart

Or

♦   If you're already working in a presentation and want to
       add a chart to a slide, open the **Insert** menu and select
       Chart. This will take you straight to the Graph window.

By default the Chart window shows a column chart; this can be changed.

To work in Graph 2000, your first step is to remove its sample data.

❶   Remove all the data by clicking on the cell at the top left
         corner and dragging the mouse to the bottom right corner
         to highlight it. Press **[Delete]** on the keyboard.

❷   Enter in your own data as shown in Figure 8.2.

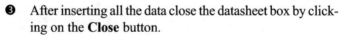

chap10 - Datasheet		A	B	C	D	E	F	
		English	Maths	Art	Geography	History	French	
1	1996	82	64	75	70	70	69	
2	1997	86	63	78	70	69	70	
3	1998	85	68	80	73	71	68	
4	1999	80	68	76	75	68	70	
5								

Figure 8.2 Entering data for a new chart

To move between the cells, click into the next cell with the mouse or
use the arrow keys on the keyboard.

It is important to insert column headings and row titles in the first cells
of columns and rows as these will be used by Graph to create labels for
the data and a legend (key) to the data.

❸   After inserting all the data close the datasheet box by click-
         ing on the **Close** button.

8.6 Formatting charts

Now that the data is stored within the graph, you will see that whilst all
the columns are in place, not all of the column labels (*English*, *Maths*,
History, etc.) are visible. This, together with other formatting functions, can be dealt with by double-clicking on to the white space around
the chart so that a placeholder appears around the chart area.

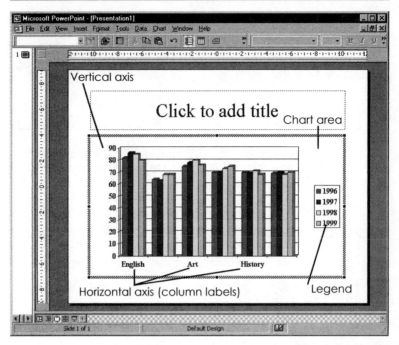

Figure 8.3 Graph 2000 after data has been inserted

With the chart selected you can now select its elements for formatting.

❶ Click onto the space between the column labels and the horizontal axis, this will select the axis.

❷ Open the **Format** menu and select **Selected Axis**.

Within the **Format Axis** dialog box (see Figure 8.4) you can make changes to the contents of that axis, e.g. column labels.

❶ Select the **Alignment** tab.

❷ Point at the red adjustment handle on the **Orientation** box and drag it until the Degree box reads 45°.

❸ Click **OK**.

Notice that when you return to the **chart** window all the **labels** on the **chart** are visible.

Figure 8.4 The **Format**
Axis dialog box

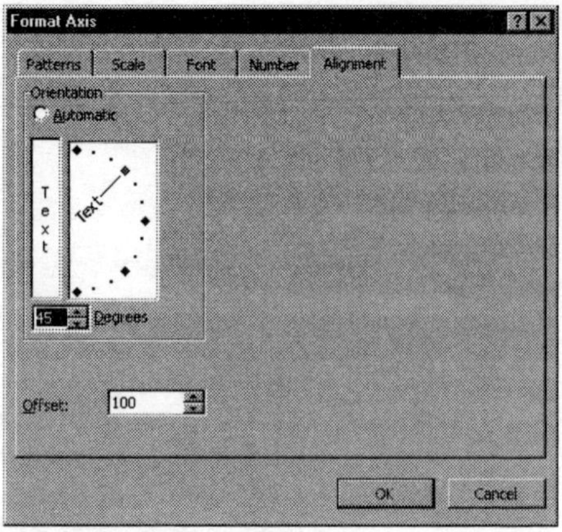

Other **Format** options make it possible to:

- Change the line colours and styles, on the **Patterns** tab.

- Show every label, or every second label, third, fourth and
  so on, on the **Scale** tab.

- Format the text, on the **Font** tab.

- Format the numbers as decimals, percentages, whole numbers, etc., on the **Number** tab.

All the tabs for the horizontal axis, can also be obtained for formatting
the vertical. The **Scale** tab, though, is used to adjust the start and end
numbers on this axis. For instance, in the example chart, our figures
are all high numbers, the lowest being 63%. The vertical axis could,
therefore, start at 60% and finish at 90% (as our largest number is 86%).

❶   Click on the vertical axis.

❷   Open the **Format** menu and click **Selected Axis**.

❸   Switch to the **Scale** tab.

❹   Click into the **Minimum** box and enter 60.

❺   Leave the **Maximum** box at 90.

❻   Change the **Major** unit to 5 (this sets the interval between
     numbers in the scale, i.e. 60, 65, 70, 75 and so on).

If your chart contains large numbers, you can make the vertical axis text easier to read by altering its **Display unit**. For example, if the values range from 1,000,000 to 50,000,000, you can display the numbers as 1 to 50 on the axis and show by a label that these are millions.

To change the Display unit:

❶ Click on to the axis you want to change.

❷ Open the **Format** menu and click **Selected Axis**

❸ Switch to the **Scale** tab.

❹ In the **Display units** box click the drop-down arrow and select the units from the list or type a numeric value.

❺ To show a label stating what the units are select the **Show display units label on chart** check box.

By selecting an individual column you can format it, to change the colour, shape, etc. Similarly, the legend can be formatted by clicking on it and using the **Format – Selected Legend** option.

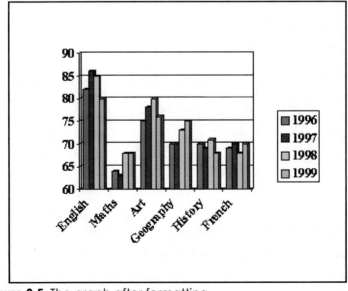

Figure 8.5 The graph after formatting

Other Graph 2000 menus

Chart

Chart Type opens a dialog box where you can choose from one of the Standard chart types or define your own on the Custom tab.

The **Chart Options...** dialog box allows you to set where and how the elements of the chart are displayed.

Format

The formatting options for the whole chart are the same as those available for individual sections.

View

The **Datasheet** option will bring the **datasheet** back on to the screen.

Zoom is not available in the Graph display. If you want to examine the chart more closely, click into the main part of the slide to revert to the normal PowerPoint window, set the Zoom level there and then double-click on the chart to reopen Graph 2000.

To change to a pie chart:

❶   Click the chart area to select it.

❷   Open the **Chart**
     menu and select
     Chart Type.

❸   Select **Pie** as the
     Chart type.

❹   Select **Exploded
     Pie** as the sub-type.

❺   Click **OK**.

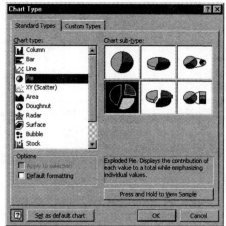

To set options:

❶ Open the **Chart** menu again and select **Chart Options…**

❷ Leave the **Titles**, as we will put a title in the title placeholder.

❸ Select the **Data Labels** tab.

❹ Turn on **Show label**. This will attach a **label** to each section of the **pie.**

❺ Click **OK**.

Sometimes a simpler display helps.

❶ Click on the line around the pie chart (the *plot area*).

❷ Open the **Format** menu and click **Selected Plot Area**.

❸ Click **None** in the **Border** section to remove the border from around the chart.

❹ Click **OK**.

❺ Click on the legend and press **[Delete]** to remove it. With the segments labelled, a legend is not necessary.

The labels need to be realigned and resized as they are currently too large for the chart.

❶ Click on one label.

❷ Open the **Format** menu and click **Selected Data Labels**.

❸ Select the **Font** tab and change the font size to 16.

❹ Select the **Alignment** tab.

❺ Realign the adjustment handle so that the labels are at an angle of 28°.

8.7 Adjusting the Datasheet

By opening the **View** menu you can select **Datasheet** so that this window opens again. This will enable you to use the **Data** menu to make changes to the data, hide columns or rows, delete or insert data.

Data

Series in rows is the current layout of the chart.

Series in columns will turn the chart round so that the years would show on the x, or horizontal axis, of a column chart.

With a particular row or column selected in the **datasheet** you can use the **Exclude Row/Column** or **Include Row/Column** commands so that the chart will be created with or without this row or column.

If you exclude a row or column from a chart you can then select it again on the datasheet and restore it to the chart by using the **Include** command.

❶ Select the chart.

❷ Open the **View** menu and select **Datasheet**.

❸ Click on the header 

to highlight the column containing data for Maths.

❹ Open the **Data** menu.

❺ Select **Exclude Row/Column**.

◆ Note how the chart has changed to exclude this column.

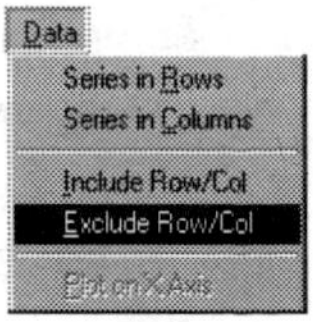

❻ Reinsert the column for maths, using **Data – Include Row/ Column**.

❼   Now click into the title placeholder and insert the title:

     A Level Results for the last four years

❽   Save and close the presentation.

DATA FROM EXCEL

By clicking on the Import File button on the Graph
toolbar you can insert a chart previously created in Excel,
or import data which will be automatically charted for you.

8.8 Organization charts

Quite often in presentations you need to show a chart depicting the
hierarchy of the organization you are promoting. This has always been
a very fiddly job, trying to get all the lines to match up, missing someone out and trying to squeeze them in somewhere, getting to the end of
the page and realizing that you actually haven't got any space left to
finish the chart!

Never fear, PowerPoint is here!! It contains Organization Chart which
will automate the otherwise tedious process of creating those charts.

A slide containing a chart can be inserted when starting a new presentation by selecting *Organization Chart* from the New Slide dialog box.
This will insert a slide which contains a title placeholder and an object
placeholder with an Organization Chart icon in the centre.

If you double-click onto this icon you will be transferred to the
Organization Chart window.

*   If you are already working in a presentation and want to
     add an Organization Chart to a slide, open the **Insert** menu,
     point to **Picture** and select **Organization Chart**. This will
     take you directly to the Chart window.

The **chart** is set up with a default layout style, which can be altered
and/or added to.

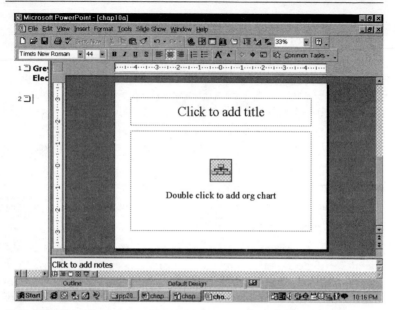

Figure 8.6 A new slide with an Organization chart placeholder

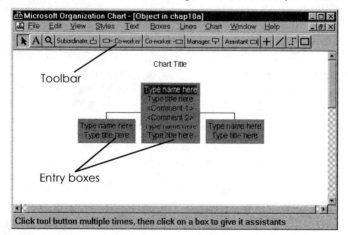

Figure 8.7 The Organization Chart window

To enter in the details:

❶   Click into the box to be completed.

❷   Click on a line, highlight its 'Type ... here' prompt and enter the name, title or comments.

❸   If prompts are not replaced or deleted, they will be displayed. If you don't want to enter anything into a line, highlight it and press **[Delete]**. The prompt will be replaced by a line name in <angle brackets> which will not appear on the finished chart.

When opening Organization Chart you will find that you are viewing it at 50% of actual size. If you click the 🔍 magnifying glass and click onto the chart, you will zoom in to see it at actual size. The 🔍 will then change to 🔡. Click this to see the whole chart. The other zoom levels can be set from the **View** menu or the keys **[F9]** to **[F12]**.

View	
Size to Window	F9
50% of Actual	F10
✓ Actual Size	F11
200% of Actual	F12
Hide Draw Tools	Ctrl+D

Comments can be added to the boxes in the chart, but be careful what you enter because these will be visible on the slide! No remarks about sacking at the end of their probationary period!

Additional levels can be added.

◆   🔲 Co-worker │ *Co-workers* are inserted on the same line as a box into which you have positioned the insertion point.

◆   │ Manager: 🔲 │ *Managers* will go above the box your insertion point is in.

◆   │ Assistant: 🔲 │ *Assistants* will come down mid-way between that position and the next level.

◆   │ Subordinate: 🔲 │ *Subordinates* will come below the box that you have selected.

You can enter text by selecting the **Text** button 🅰 and clicking anywhere on the chart window. If you click onto the text at a later time a placeholder will appear around it and formatting changes can be made.

The following practical exercise will create an organization chart for a firm. Use the names and descriptions as given, or substitute your own if you prefer.

❶ Create a new presentation and select the *Organization chart* option from the New Slide dialog box.

❷ Double click on the Organization Chart icon to open the Organization Chart window.

❸ Position the insertion point into the top box.

Highlight the '*Type name here*' and enter: '**Clive Grey**'

Highlight the Title prompt and enter: '**Partner**'

❹ Select the **co-worker** button.

❺ Click into the box containing *Clive Grey* so that a co-worker box appears alongside it.

Click into the Name line and type: '**Gerald Minister**'

In the Title line, type: '**Partner**'

❻ Select one of the boxes on the line below *Clive Grey*.

❼ Open the **Edit** menu and select **Clear**.

❽ In the two remaining boxes enter: '**Stephen Minister**' and '**John Essex**'

Your chart should now look like this:

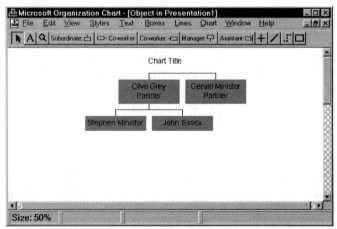

Figure 8.8 The Chart after entering the first items

Check it, and correct if necessary before you go on to complete the chart.

❶ Add a **Sub-ordinate** box under *Stephen Minister*.

❷ Type in: 'Simon Hunt' and 'Apprentice'

❸ Click the **Assistant** button and add a box under *Clive Grey*.

❹ Enter the text: 'Sheila Burrows' and 'Admin Assistant'

❺ Highlight the **Chart title** and delete it, replacing it with:
Grey & Minister Electrical Engineers

Drawing lines

At the moment the chart shows that the **assistant** works for only one partner. Use the **Show Draw Tools** command on the **View** menu to add these tools to the toolbar. You can then use them to create new lines between boxes.

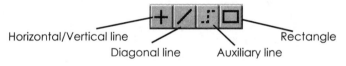

Horizontal/Vertical line   Rectangle

Diagonal line   Auxiliary line

In this instance we need to use the **auxiliary** line as this will form a line with angles so that it will neatly join the second partner to the assistant. When using lines it is important that each end touches the boxes to be joined.

❶ Select the **auxiliary** line and drag it from the second part-ner box to the admin assistant box. The line is a faint dot-ted line at the moment, but should be a solid black line.

❷ Open **Lines** menu.

❸ Select **Style**.

❹ Select the solid line.

The background of the chart and of individual boxes, and each text item can all be recoloured if required.

To change the background colour of the chart:

❶   Open the **Chart** menu.

❷   Select **Background Color**.

❸   Select a colour and click **OK**.

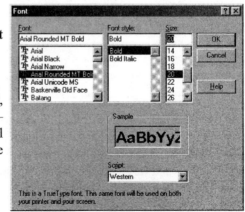

To change the colour of the boxes:

❶   Click on one of the *partner* boxes.

◆   If you want the other *partner* box to be the same colour,
    hold down **[Shift]** and click on the box to select it also.

❷   Open the **Boxes** menu.

❸   Click on **Color…**

❹   Select a colour and click **OK**.

◆   Change the colour of the other boxes in the same way.

To set the font colour in boxes:

❶   Select the boxes.

❷   Open the **Text** menu.

❸   Select **Color…**

❹   Select a colour and click **OK**.

To change the font of the title or of text in boxes:

❶   Select the text.

❷   Open the **Text**
    menu.

❸   Select **Font….**

❹   Choose a **Font**,
    Style and **Size** –
    the **Sample** will
    help you choose
    a format.

❺   Click **OK**.

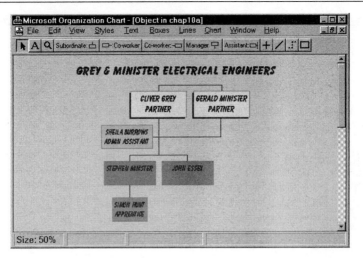

Figure 8.9 The completed Chart

CLICK AND DRAG SELECTION

By clicking on 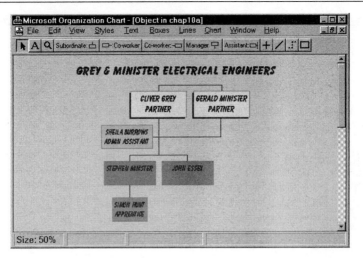 you can draw a box over the whole chart, to select it. Position the mouse pointer at the top left corner of the window and drag the mouse down to the bottom right corner. With the whole chart selected you can make formatting changes that will affect everything.

Chart styles

The style of the chart is fairly straightforward but this can be changed from the default settings to an alternative selection stored within the **Styles** menu.

❶ Select all the boxes.

❷ Open the **Styles** menu.

❸ Click an option in the **Groups** section (the top two lines) to change the layout.

♦ The other options can be used on selected Assistant and Co-Manager boxes to set their layout.

When you have finished editing and formatting your chart, return to PowerPoint to see how it looks on the slide.

❶ Open the **File** menu.

❷ Select **Close and Return to** *file name*.

If you select **Update** *file name*, your slide will be updated with any changes made in the chart but the Organization Chart window will remain open on your screen.

♦ If you want to edit the **chart**, after return to the slide, double-click on it to open the Organization Chart window.

The slide itself has a placeholder for a title, so the one typed onto the chart isn't needed. It could be deleted or cut and pasted into the title placeholder or the slide.

❶ Double-click on the chart.

❷ **Cut** the title and **paste** it into the slide's title placeholder

❸ Highlight the title.

❹ Open the **Edit** menu and select **Cut.**

❺ Open the **File** menu and select **Close and return to the presentation**.

❻ Click on placeholder.

❼ Open the **Edit** menu and select **Paste**.

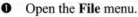

SUMMARY

In this chapter we have looked at the various applications which are compatible with PowerPoint, learning:

✓ How to import or copy/cut and paste data from other applications or files into a presentation.

✓ How to use Graph 2000 within a presentation.

✓ How to set up an Organization Chart on a slide.

9 | **USING THE INTERNET**

AIMS OF THIS CHAPTER

In this chapter our aim is to show how you can create presentations suitable for putting onto the World Wide Web, or sending as e-mails. We will also be learning how to use PowerPoint as a means of conducting interactive meetings over the Internet.

9.1 The Internet and PowerPoint

With the world decreasing in size rapidly because of the expansion of international communication facilities, it is no longer necessary to arrange a meeting with your colleagues weeks in advance, organize a venue with lunch and coffee, or incur the cost of travel expenses and maybe hotel accommodation. Now all that is needed is for each meeting member to be on-line (connected to the Internet) and to be advised through the on-line meeting facility, in Outlook, of a date and time they should be on-line and have NetMeeting open to participate. Although there will not be any verbal communication, the host of the meeting (i.e., you) can communicate through PowerPoint in NetMeeting by creating a presentation to be shown. You can add comments to the presentation or you can arrange for one of the other participants to add comments.

You can use Outlook to broadcast a presentation to an audience over the Internet, or the company intranet, which may be large, as long as it doesn't need active involvement. All the audience needs to receive and view it is an Internet browser such as Internet Explorer.

If it is not a meeting through the Internet that you want but a Web page to be viewed by a wider audience, then that can also be done through PowerPoint. Web pages are constructed using Hypertext Mark-up Language (HTML). In PowerPoint however, you can create a new, or use an existing presentation and save it as a Web Page. It will be converted into HTML so it can be published on the World Wide Web.

PowerPoint presentations, like files from any of the Office applications can be e-mailed directly from the application or as attachments.

9.2 On-line meetings

It is possible now to communicate over the Internet or corporate intranets by using the NetMeeting application. This has been integrated into the the Office 2000 suite, and allows you to share information with other users at different sites worldwide. NetMeeting works in real time, in other words there is no delay and all participants will be communicating with each other at the same time.

To arrange a meeting:

❶   Open the **Tools** menu.

❷   Point to **On-line Collabora-tion** and then select whether the meeting should take place now or be scheduled for another time.

If you are invited to join someone else's meeting you will receive a message in Outlook asking you to join, or reminding you of a meeting. On accepting this request, if the meeting is on-going, the on-line toolbar and presentation will appear on your screen. You should have NetMeeting running on your computer to be able to join the meeting.

If you choose to schedule a meeting for a later date or time, Outlook will come up on your screen with details to be completed in respect of the time and date of the meeting, and its subject, this information will be sent to the other requested participants. Outlook will remind the participants before the meeting that it will be starting shortly so that they can load NetMeeting and prepare themselves. At the time of the meeting all participants should be in NetMeeting in order to participate or view what is happening.

As the *host*, that is the person who has organized the meeting, you will have overall control of the presentation, Whiteboard and Chat facilities.

◆   The **Whiteboard** is a feature in NetMeeting which opens a window in which on-line participants can demonstrate their points with the use of text, objects, shapes, copying, pasting or deleting objects.

◆   **Chat** is also a NetMeeting feature and when it is selected a window opens where participants of the meeting can type and send messages to each other.

The participants of the meeting can only use these if the host turns on collaboration. This facility enables all participants to be actively involved in the meeting. If collaboration is turned on everyone can add comments or diagrams to the Whiteboard, or edit each other's. All participants can also communicate with each other through the Chat facility by typing their messages or comments. All participants can take turns to make comments or changes, and during this time the participant who is editing will have control of the presentation. Whilst collaboration is turned on the host will not have use of the insertion point.

It is not really feasible to take you through the steps of running an on-line meeting here, but should you wish to try it out with someone, here are some of the instructions you might need to run an on-line meeting:

The Online Meeting toolbar

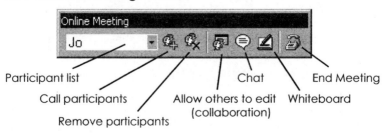

If you are the host:

- To turn on collaboration – click on **Allow others to edit** on the on-line meeting toolbar.

- To regain control of the meeting whilst collaboration is turned on, click anywhere in the presentation.

- To turn off collaboration – take control of the meeting and click on **Allow others to edit** again, or press **[Escape]**.

- To end a meeting click on the **End meeting** button.

- To be able to see exactly who is participating in the meeting click on the **Participants list** on the on-line meeting toolbar.

- To remove a participant from the meeting, select the name from the participant list and click **Remove participants**.

- As the host you can open the Whiteboard by clicking on **Display whiteboard**.

If you are a participant in a meeting in which you are not the host and you want to take control of the presentation you should double-click anywhere in the presentation the first time you want to take over. Any time after that you only need to click once into the presentation. Obviously, as in a face-to-face meeting, you can't just grab the floor when you want to – ask the host, or the group, first.

Although there is the Online Meeting toolbar available this can only be used by the host of the meeting. If you are a participant and wish to have greater control of the meeting, you should work directly in the NetMeeting progam by opening it directly from Windows 98 rather than through Office.

Participants must also work directly in NetMeeting if they want to have access to the Whiteboard or Chat. These cannot be accessed if users are working in NetMeeting through Office.

9.3 Broadcasting a presentation

Using broadcasting facilities can be an alternative to arranging a meeting through NetMeeting. If you do not require the participation of your audience, or if the audience is particularly large, then broadcasting is the most efficient way of getting the message across to them.

It is possible to include video and audio clips in your presentation when using the broadcasting facility. NetShow, however, is required if you wish to show video clips in the presentation, or if your broadcast is to more than 15 people.

A broadcast can be set up through PowerPoint or through Outlook, in the same way that you would schedule a meeting.

A reminder to your audience will be sent 15 minutes prior to the start time. It includes an action button, which when pressed, takes them to the *broadcast lobby page* in the browser (Internet Explorer). The lobby page will contain outline details for the presentation, such as the name of the author, the title of the presentation, any supporting comments from the author and a countdown to the start time. The broadcast will start automatically when it's ready.

Here's how to run a broadcast.

The options for showing a broadcast need to be set only once, from then on any broadcast you wish to show will follow the same settings.

To set up and schedule a broadcast:

❶ Open the presentation. On the **Slide Show** menu, point to **Online Broadcast...** and select **Set Up and Schedule...**

❷ Select **Set up and schedule a new broadcast**, then click **OK**.

❸ Select the **Description** tab and enter in the details that you want the lobby page to contain.

❹ Check the settings on the **broadcast settings** tab. If they aren't correct, set them up for your participants' uses. (Check with your system administrator what these should be, if necessary.)

❺   Click **OK.** Now you're ready to arrange the broadcast.

❻   Click **Schedule Broadcast**. If you're working with Out-
     look then follow the processes for this software to arrange
     a broadcast. (See Outlook's Help for more details.) If you
     are not working through Outlook then enter the broadcast
     date and time in the message. When the recipient sees the
     message they will also see the URL of the broadcast site.

To be able to start a presentation to show it as a broadcast over the
Internet, or intranet, you need to:

◆   Open the presentation in PowerPoint and select the **Slide
     Show** menu, point to **Online Broadcast** and select **Begin
     Broadcast**. Your presentation will be found at the server
     location that you designated when setting it up.

9.4 Creating Web pages

Nowadays, anyone can create a Web page or site (a set of pages with
links from its home page) and publish it on the World Wide Web.

Before starting, check that your Internet service provider offers space
for Web pages. (Most do these days). You need to find out the URL
(Uniform Resource Locator) for your page. You should create a web
folder, using the wizard, and insert the URL as the folder name.

❶   In **My Computer**, open **Web Folders**.

You can also find
Web Folders in
Windows Explorer
– it will be at the
bottom of the
folder display

❷ Double-click Add Web Folder to start the wizard.

❸ Enter the URL of your home page. The wizard will run
    Dial Up Networking to go on-line and check the URL.
    Follow the prompts to set up your Web folder.

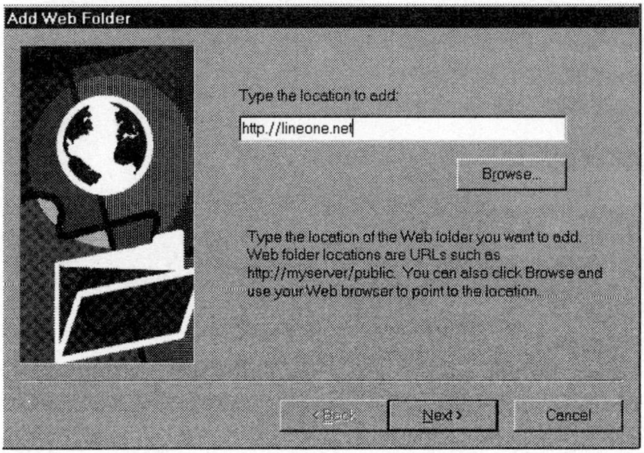

Add Web Folder

Type the location to add:

http://lineone.net

Browse...

Type the location of the Web folder you want to add.
Web folder locations are URLs such as
http://myserver/public. You can also click Browse and
use your Web browser to point to the location.

< Back   Next >   Cancel

Figure 9.1 Using the Add Web Folder wizard

Usually, to create a web page you would use an HTML editor or write
it directly in HTML. This book, however, is not going to show you
how to create a web page using HTML! Instead, you will see how a
PowerPoint presentation can be converted into a web page.

To create a web page from a presentation you simply open it and then
save it again as a web page into the previously created web folder.

❶ Open PowerPoint.

❷ Click into **Open an existing presentation** (or choose the
    presentation name from those listed).

❸ In the **Open** dialog box, select the folder which contains
    your presentation from the **Look in** drop-down list.

❹ Select the name from the list and click **Open**.

❺ Open the **File** menu and select **Save As**.

❻　For the **Save as type:** select *Web Page.* (Note how it is now slightly different from the usual Save as dialog box).

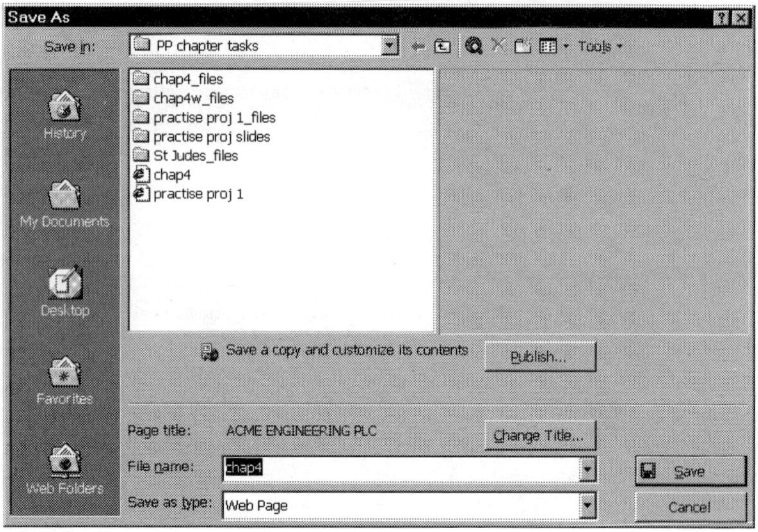

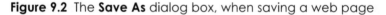

Figure 9.2 The **Save As** dialog box, when saving a web page

❼　In the **Save in** drop-down box select *Web folders* and select the folder into which the file should be saved.

❽　In the **File name** box, edit the name, if necessary.

You'll see that the web page has been given a **Page title**, that of the title slide. This will appear on the title bar of the viewers' browser. If you want to change it, click on **Change Title...** and edit as required.

❶　Click on **Publish**, and at the **Publish as Web Page** dialog box (see next page), edit the settings as necessary.

❷　After making changes click **Publish**. You are now able to see how your presentation will be viewed over the Internet!

Changes can be made to the web page after it has been published by updating the source file, i.e. the original presentation, and saving it as a web page again over the top of the previously saved version.This will ensure that all the changes are included in the new web page.

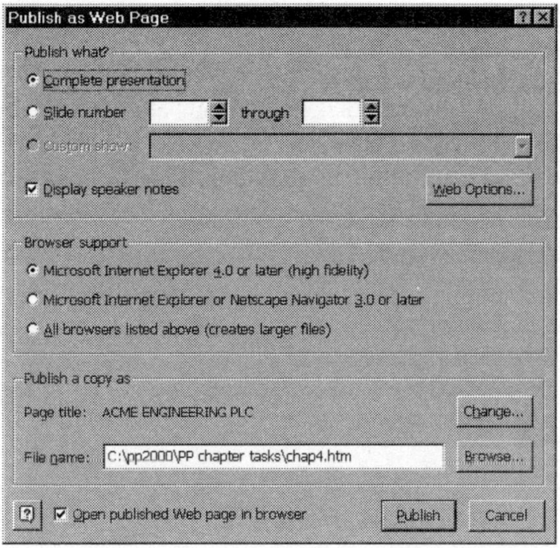

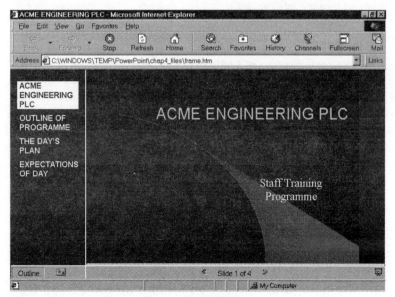

Figure 9.3 The **Publish as Web Page** dialog box – tick *Open published Web page in browser* to view it after publishing

Figure 9.4 Title slide of the presentation as a Web page

9.5 Discussions in web page presentations

With your presentation converted to a web page it is possible to set it up so that other users can make comments about it, and these can be responded to, by you or others, in the form of a discussion. The comments are threaded together so that they lead on from each other and make more sense to all users rather than just those in the discussion.

Web discussions can be accessed through the **Tools – Online Collaboration** command but are only available to those users who have Office Server Extensions set up on their computer network. Assuming you have a systems administrator who has set up the server extensions you will be able to obtain the necessary discussion server details to take part in a discussion.

9.6 Hyperlinks in web pages

Hyperlinks are discussed in detail in Chapter 11, but briefly they are buttons, text or images, that when clicked take the user from the current slide to the next, or back or to somewhere else altogether, for instance a file in a different application.

They can also be used on web pages in exactly the same way. If you want to send the viewer to another file then a hyperlink can be set up to take them to a second presentation, or the Excel spreadsheet that holds the figures upon which your presentation is based. Hyperlinks can also be used to take the user to the mail software and send an e-mail back to you. For instance if you want responses to a particular slide you can create a text frame on the slide somewhere, enter your name or e-mail address and set this as a hyperlink so that when viewers click on it they will be taken directly to the mail window to send a message.

❶   Open the file you previously saved as a web page and go to the first slide.

❷   Select the **Text tool** from the Drawing toolbar and click onto the slide.

❸   Type in your **e-mail address**, or your name and a note to indicate that this is an e-mail link.

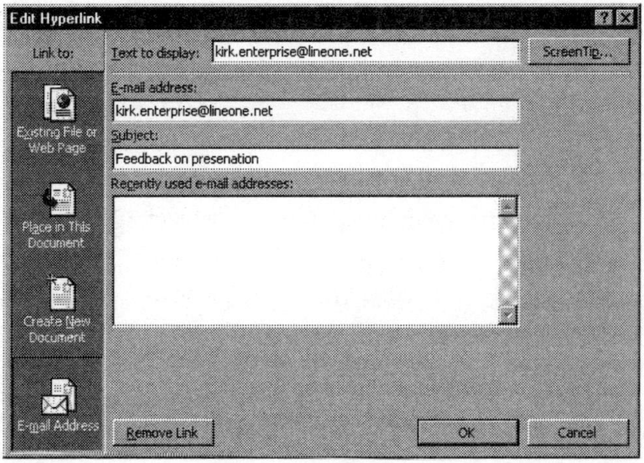

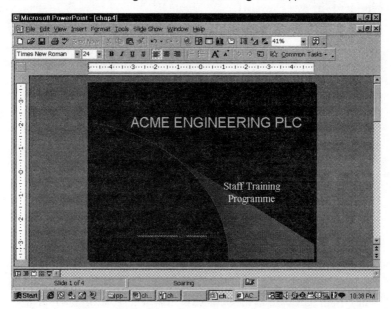

Figure 9.5 Creating an E-mail address hyperlink – in this example, the full e-mail link has been used as the screen text. You could instead use your normal name or any text. What matters is that the e-mail address is given when defining the hyperlink.

Figure 9.6 Slide view after the hyperlink has been added

❹   Select the text, then open the **Insert** menu and select
    Hyperlink.

❺   From the **Link to** list in the **Insert Hyperlink** dialog box,
    select **E-mail address**.

❻   In the **E-mail address** line, key in your address and in the
    Subject line enter an appropriate subject. Click **OK**.

To check that the hyperlink is working properly, change to Slide Show
view. When you move the mouse over the hyperlink, the *mailto* link
will be displayed in a pop-up box. When you click on it, the e-mail
message window will open so that you can send an e-mail to the address in the **To:** box.

9.7 E-mailing a presentation

You can send your presentation as an e-mail from within PowerPoint
by opening the **File** menu, pointing to **Send To** and selecting **Mail
recipient (as attachment)** – see Figure 9.7.

If you want to send the presentation to a number of recipients then you
can select **Routing Recipient** as the **Send To** option. This enables you
to specify if it should be sent to one after the other or all at once.

To send the same presentation to a number of people:

❶   Open the **Send to** option in the **File** menu and select **Rout-
    ing Recipient…**. The **Add Routine Slip** dilalog box will
    open (see Figure 9.8).

❷   In the **To** list select a recipient and click **Add Slip.**

❸   Repeat to add all the recipients.

❹   Type in a message to go with the presentation and specify
    whether they should all go at once or one after the other.

❺   Click **Route**.

Obviously, the same presentation can be sent as an attachment through
your e-mail software in the same way that you send anything else.

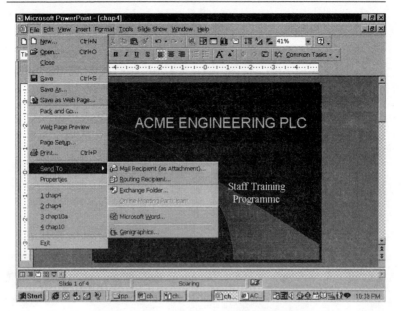

Figure 9.7 Sending a presentation via e-mail.

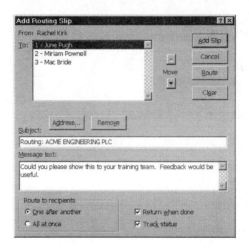

Figure 9.8 The routing dialog box

FILE SIZES AND TRANSFER TIMES

You should also think about file sizes and transfer times. Simple presentations are roughly between 20Kb and 50Kb per slide. If the presentation contains audio and video clips, it could well run to several megabytes in total. When sent by e-mail, files have to be converted into a special form which makes them about half as big again. For example, a 10-slide presentation containing a 5 minute audio clip would probably be over 3Mb, or 5Mb when mailed. This would take nearly half an hour for you to send – and just as long for your recipients to receive.

SUMMARY

We have covered the following in this chapter:

✓ Working cooperatively with Online meetings.

✓ Broadcasting a presentation over the Internet or intranet.

✓ Converting a presentation into a web page and adding e-mail hyperlinks.

✓ Sending presentations via e-mail.

10 ANIMATION AND SOUNDS

AIMS OF THIS CHAPTER

In this chapter we will be looking at various animation and sound techniques which we can apply to our presentations, in order to enhance them.

10.1 Transitions and timings

With PowerPoint you can bring your presentation to life by creating effects that link the slides together, insert sound and video clips into individual slides and create animated effects that set the way the text and graphics appear on the screen or projector.

First we're going to look at transition and timings. These establish the way one slide leads into another. You might have noticed, when using Slide Show view in previous chapters of this book, that as a slide moved to the next it jumped rather abruptly when a key was pressed or the mouse clicked. This can be changed so that the new slide can appear on your screen more automatically and smoothly.

By setting your own transitions you can dictate how the presentation moves along, the speed at which it moves and the sound effects for transition and whether or not you set it up to progress automatically with time delays, or manually.

❶ Open an existing practice presentation or create a new one. It should have at least five slides.

❷ Set a different background colour for each slide.

It is possible to work on transition effects in any view. If using Normal, Slide or Outline view, you need to select **Slide Transition** from the **Slide Show** menu. If you are in Slide Sorter view you can also use the **Slide Transition** button 🔲 on the Slide Sorter toolbar.

❶   Change your view to Slide view.

❷   Open the **Slide Show** menu and select **Slide Transition**.

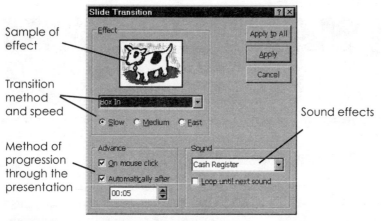

Figure 10.1 The **Slide Transition** dialog box

The dialog box displays an image of 'Spot' the dog which is meant to be a sample slide to demonstrate the result of the different transitions. By clicking on the drop-down arrow in the transition box you will see a list of many alternative transitions.

❶   Click on the transitions box and select *Dissolve* from the list.

❷   Set the speed of the transition to *Slow*.

❸   In **Advance**, click into *Automatically after*.

❹   Change the time to 00:05. This the interval between slides.

❺   In the **Sound** box click on the drop-down arrow and select the *Applause* effect.

❻   Click **Apply** to set these transition effects for the slide.

By selecting **Apply** the effects will only affect the one slide. If you select **Apply to all** then the same effects will be set for each slide in the presentation.

By clicking on the **Slide Show** button , your slide will open on the screen with the effects you've created. To return to Slide view, click on the right mouse button and select **End show** or press **[Escape]**.

Move on to Slide 2:

❶   Follow the above steps to create a different set of transition effects for this slide.

❷   Repeat to create different effects for Slides 3 and 4.

Try to make your transition effect link in with the sound effect, for instance *Cover Right* and *Screeching Brakes*. Sometimes it is easier to choose the sound and then decide on the transition effect.

❶   Change the view to **Slide Sorter** view .

❷   Select the transition effect from the drop-down menu on the toolbar.

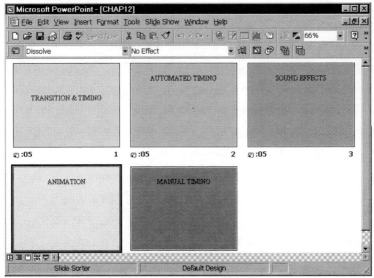

Figure 10.2 Setting transitions in Slide Sorter view

Rather frustratingly, you can't select any of the other transition effects from the Slide Sorter toolbar. You need to click on the **Slide Transition** button to continue setting up your transition effects.

❶ Click on the **Slide Transition** button 🔲.

❷ Change the timing and sound, then select **Apply**.

❸ Select the first slide.

❹ Click on **Slide Show** button 🔲 to view the complete show.

If you don't select the first slide before going to Slide Show view the slide show will start with whichever slide is selected.

10.2 Animation effects

It is not just the transition between slides that can be changed to create a smoother, more professional appearance. The effect of the text and objects on slides themselves can be altered so that their appearance has an impact on the audience. At the moment, text, images and sounds on a slide appear with the slide, we can change this so that they appear separately, line by line, with the lists or objects appearing in specific order all with sound effects in the background. All of these can be set so that it happens automatically within a set time.

The animation of slide contents relates to the text, objects or clip art.

❶ Select or create a slide containing a title and some clip art, as in Figure 10.3.

Now we're going to set the animation of this slide so that the text and the graphic 'fly' onto the slide.

❷ Make sure you're in Normal or Slide view.

❸ Open the **Slide Show** menu and select **Custom animation...**

❹ Click on the **Effects** tab.

❺ In the **Check to animate slide objects** box click into the object you will be animating, e.g. *Title 1*.

Figure 10.3 The slide before animating

❻ In the **Entry Animation and Sound** drop-down menus select a sound effect and entry effect for the title.

❼ The **Introduce text** box provides the options of text coming onto the screen *All at once*, a *Word* or a *Letter* at a time. Select one of the choices from this drop-down menu.

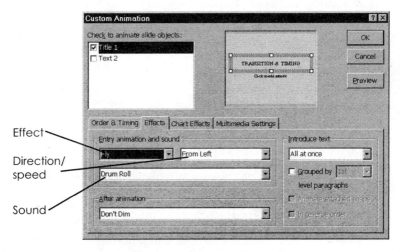

Figure 10.4 The **Custom Animation** dialog box

- ◆ Whatever selection you've made you can preview at each
  step by clicking on the **Preview** button.

The **After animation** box will probably display *Don't Dim*. This will
ensure that the object or text remains on the screen after the animation
is completed. If you select any of the other options, the selected text or
object will do as the option implies, either hide when the animation is
complete, hide when the mouse button is clicked or change colour.

- ❶ Leave settings for **After animation** on *Don't Dim*.

- ❷ Select *Picture frame 2* from the **Check to animate slide
  objects** box and repeat the steps to animate the object.

- ❸ Click **OK** to close the dialog box and return to the presentation.

- ❹ Repeat the above steps to set up the animation effects for
  Slide 2, using a different range of animations.

Having closed the Custom Animation dialog box you can preview the
effects set up on that individual slide:

- ❶ Open the **Slide Show** menu.

- ❷ Click **Animation Preview**.

This will bring a small preview window up on your screen in which
you can view what you've done to the slide. To remove this window
click its Close button.

When using the custom animation effects, you can set up the slides so
that the text, graphics, objects and so forth can be brought on to the
screen in the order that you dictate. For instance, you might want a
picture to come on to the screen first followed by the title, and then the
text, or you make the answer to a question appear before the question!

- ❶ Move on to Slide 3 and open the **Custom Animation**
  dialog box from the **Slide Show** menu.

- ❷ Click on the **Effects** tab.

- ❸ Select *Title 1* in the **Check to animate slide objects** box
  and set up the animation effects for this.

❹   Repeat for the *Text 2*.

❺   Having set up both parts of the slide, click on the **Order & Timing** tab.

At the moment the order of the slide will be set to the default of going from the first item through to the last. Here, you need to change things around so that the text comes on to the screen first followed by the title.

❶   In the **Animation order** box select the object you want to refer to, i.e. *Text 2.*

❷   Click an arrow to move this object up or down in the list of slide objects. In this instance, click ⬆ to move the selected object above the *Title 1* object.

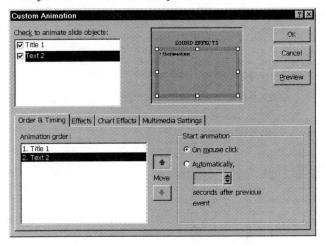

Figure 10.5 Setting the animation order

INSTANT ANIMATIONS

If you don't want to go to the lengths of setting each individual component of the animation effects you can select the object, or placeholder on a slide that you want to animate and choose an option from the list of **Preset Animations** in the **Slide Show** menu.

Also within this tab you can set a delay between each object coming on to the screen. So, if you set the timing for the current slide to 10 seconds *Title 1* would come onto the screen 10 seconds after *Text 2*.

❶   Repeat the steps above for Slide 3 and change the animation and order and timing for Slide 4.

❷   In Slide 5 set up the animation effects, bearing in mind that it's the last slide in this short presentation.

❸   Whilst in Slide 5 add clip art to show that it is the end of a dynamic presentation – a firework or champagne cork?

❹   Select **Custom Animation** from **Slide Show** menu. Go to the **Effects** tab and set up the effects for the clip art.

❺   Change the **Order and Timing** so that the clip art comes on to the screen between the title and the text.

If you want to be really impressive you could ungroup the clip art and set up the animation, order and timing for each individual element!

◆   Charts can also be animated using the **Custom animation** dialog box. For these select the **Chart Effects** tab, not the **Effects** tab.

10.3 Slide Timings

We have seen in the steps above how to set up timings for automated presentations. The only problem with doing these is that if you get stopped for a question during your presentation it will upset the whole show as the slides will carry on despite you taking a bit longer over one slide than you anticipated. You can overcome this by pressing **[Escape]** to interrupt the presentation, but this would return your screen to the working screen that would disturb the flow of the presentation and break the concentration of the audience.

Alternatively you can use the **Rehearse timings** option which will allow you to record timings as you rehearse. This will enable you to talk your way through the presentation, make allowances for any interruptions and so have a more accurately timed presentation.

The other option is to set up the slides so that the timing is manual, i.e. the show will move to the next slide when you click the mouse button. This is probably the most useful if you are expecting a lot of questions throughout the presentation rather than a question time at the end.

To use the rehearse timing facility:

❶   Select **Rehearse Timings** from the **Slide Show** menu. The Rehearsal toolbar will appear and the timing for the show will start immediately.

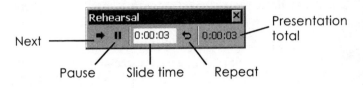

❷   Click on the **Next** button to move to the next object or slide to be brought on to the screen.

❸   At the end of the slide show, a dialog box will appear asking if you want to accept the timings recorded, click **Yes**.

❹   Select the first slide and click the Slide Show view button to view the presentation.

◆   If you want slides to move on either when you click the mouse (useful if you've set your delay for too long) or automatically, select both options in the **Slide Transitions** option in **Slide Show** menu. An action button (see Chapter 11) will be added to the slide. This can be clicked when you want to move to the next slide.

Manual control

To run the slide show using the manual transition option select **On mouse click** in the Slide Transitions dialog box.

10.4 Movies and sounds

What we've covered so far in this chapter will make a substantial difference to your presentation, really bringing it to life.

You can also add sounds, video clips and music from sources other than PowerPoint, e.g. your folders, clip art files or CDs. Audio and video clips are inserted into slides from the source file, in just the same way as images and text files. Once you've positioned a clip, you can set up and run the presentation automatically, including the imported sounds or video clips when you move to relevant slide. Alternatively, it can be set up to run manually and for the sound or video to start when you click the icon on the slide.

- If PowerPoint can't convert a sound, music or video clip to run as an object, it can be played through the Media Player in Windows 98.

- You need speakers and a sound card on your system to play sound and music.

Sound, music and video clips are either played automatically or by using icons. These appear on your slide for you to play the sound or video track when you are ready.

To insert music, sound or video it is the same process, using the **Movies and Sounds** from the **Insert** menu.

You can insert sound or videos from the Microsoft Clipart gallery by choosing **Sound/Movie from Gallery** and locating and inserting the appropriate file. To insert sound or video from another source select **Sound/Movie from File**, locate the folder that holds the object and double-click on it.

A message then appears on the screen asking you to specify if you want the sound/video to play automatically when you go to the slide, or if it should wait until you click on the ◀ icon. Select **Yes** or **No** depending on your requirements.

Sound can also be added to a slide show through your CD drive. If you want to add a track from a CD for instance:

❶   Select the slide to which it should be added.

❷   Open the **Insert** menu, point to **Movies and Sounds**, and
    select **Play CD Audio Track…**.

❸   Select the track and timings that you want to play, e.g.
    start on track 3, stop on track 4, play for 15 seconds.

    You can only set the start and stop timings for the track if
    you are selecting one other than the first track. The start
    time will be the time that the track you are playing, e.g.
    track 3, will start and the stop time will be when you want
    it to stop. For instance if you want to hear 15 seconds, you
    need to add 15 to the start time.

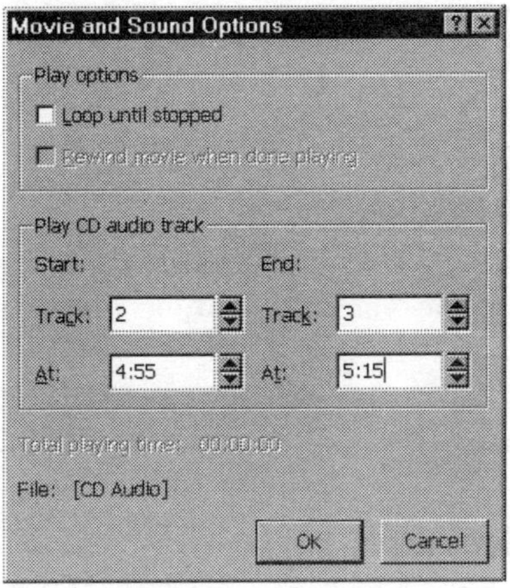

Figure 10.6 Setting the playing time for a CD clip

❹   Click **OK**. The CD button 📀 will appear on the slide.

❺   The message asking confirmation manual or automatic
    play will appear. Select **No**.

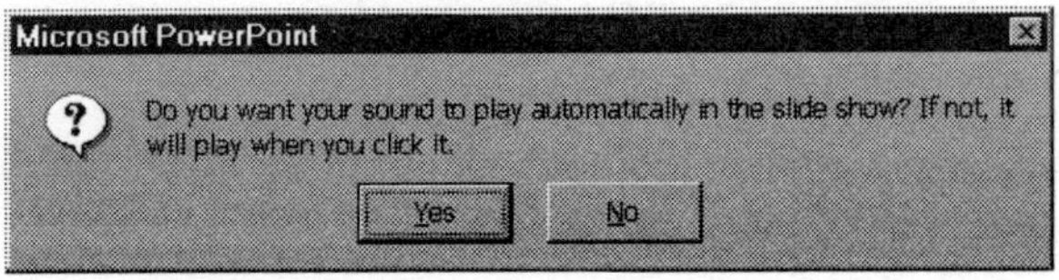

If you set the sound or CD to be turned on manually, a tiny icon will appear in the centre of the slide. You can resize it and reposition it to fit in with the rest of the slide. To preview the sound or video in Normal, or Slide view, double-click on the icon.

* Run the slide show.

The animation options can be set up for sound, music or video as well as the text and objects on your slides. To set the options for the CD track that you've just created:

❶ Bring the slide with the CD track on to your screen.

❷ Select **Custom Animation** from the **Slide Show** menu.

❸ Open the **Multimedia Settings** tab.

❹ Tick *Media* in the **Check to animate slide objects** box.

❺ Specify that you want to keep the slide show running and for it to stop playing after two slides.

❻ Click on **OK**.

* If you want to make further changes to the CD track settings then click on **More Options** to return to the CD settings dialog box.

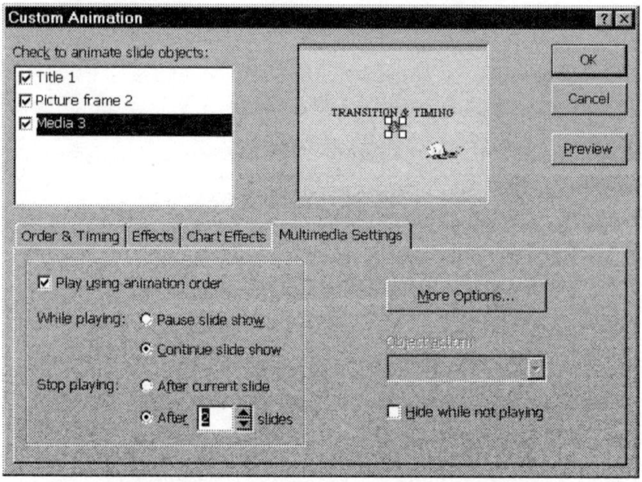

Figure 10.7 Setting the animation options for an audio clip

10.5 Narration

Narration recorded on to a presentation can be very useful for a number of purposes, e.g. when showing a self-running presentation at an exhibition or when sending it to be viewed at a different site. In theory it could also be added to a Web presentation, but unless you use special technology, the whole sound file would have to download before your viewer could hear anything, and at around 10Kb per second (for 'Telephone quality' sound), files tend to be very large. This is also worth remembering if you intend to e-mail the presentation. A 5-minute narration would be around 3Mb and take up to half an hour to download!

A narration can be recorded in advance of the show, or whilst the presentation is progressing. This way you will be able to include audience comments and responses as well as the narration. This method could be very useful for evaluation purposes following a presentation.

Narration can be made for the whole presentation or for individual slides. You should be aware, though, that when you record a narrative on to a slide any other sounds will be lost.

To record a narration for a whole presentation ensure you have a sound card and microphone connected to your computer.

❶   From the **Slide Show** menu select **Record Narration**.

◆   You will see a dialog box indicating the length of time you can record, this will alter depending on the amount of disk space is available on your computer.

- If you are using the microphone for the first time click on **Set microphone level** so as to make sure you will be heard clearly, follow any on-screen instructions.

❷ To record a straightforward narration click on **OK**.

- This will create an embedded narration, i.e. it will be part of the presentation and any changes must be done here.

❸ Alternatively you could select the **Link narrations in** check box so that the narration is stored as a separate, but linked, file. This gives better performance.

- Having clicked on **OK**, advance through the presentation recording your narrative. You will find that you will have to advance manually through the presentation, pressing the mouse button or an arrow key to move on to the next step.

- When you reach the end a dialog box will appear asking if you want to save the timings made during the narration, to save them click **Yes,** to ignore them click **No**.

Bearing in mind the fact that the narration will wipe out other sounds you might find it more useful to do recordings for individual slides, where they are specifically appropriate:

❶ Make sure your microphone is connected and display the slide to which you want to add narrative.

❷ Select **Movies and Sounds** from the **Insert** menu.

❸ Click **Record Sound**.

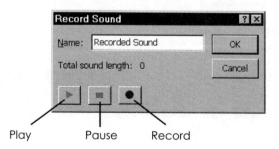

❹   When you're ready to record your narration click the **Record** button and speak into the microphone.

❺   On completion click **OK** to finish.

A sound icon will appear in the slide to which it is added and unless you set up the narration to turn on automatically you will need to click on the sound icon to run the message.

To animate the sound:

❶   Click on the sound icon.

❷   Open the **Slide Show** menu and select **Custom Animations...**

❸   Make the necessary changes in **Multimedia Settings**, **Effects** and **Order & Timings** tabs.

To delete a narration or sound from a slide, click on the sound icon on the slide and press **[Delete]**.

It is possible to run the slide show without the narration and without the need to delete it. Open the **Slide Show** menu and select **Set Up Show...** In the dialog box, tick the **Show without narration** option.

SUMMARY

In this chapter we have covered:

✓ Setting the transitions between slides.

✓ Display text and objects using animation effects.

✓ Setting the slide timings.

✓ inserting movies and sounds into slides.

✓ Recording a narration for the whole presentation of selected slides.

11 | THE PRESENTATION

AIMS OF THIS CHAPTER

In this chapter we will be discussing the different ways in presenting and managing your slide show, ensuring a smoothly run presentation. We will look at how to manipulate a presentaion whilst running, making jumps between slides possible, as well as self-running shows. This chapter also looks at running the show from a computer other than the one the show was created on, and how to make notes whilst it is running.

11.1 Viewing a slide show

Presentations created in PowerPoint can be viewed in three different ways. Each method of viewing can be found in the **Set Up Show** dialog box. They are *Presented by speaker* (full screen), *Browsed by an individual* (window) or *Browsed at kiosk* (full screen).

The first option, *Presented by speaker* shows a full screen presentation, either on the computer monitor, or on a projector. This method is usually supported by a speaker who has control of the presentation. Whilst using this mode, you can record a narration of the presentation and responses and make notes of it using Meeting Minder.

The second method, *Browsed by an individual* will show a slide on the screen but it won't fill the whole screen. The purpose of this view is for it to be used on the World Wide Web or over a company network to provide information to staff. The presentation is interactive allowing the viewer to copy or print the presentation, or even edit it! These actions, together with progressing, or returning through the presentation can be managed through the use of the right mouse button. Or by moving through the presentation with the scroll bar or **[Page Up]** and **[Page Down]** keys.

The third option *Browsed at a kiosk* uses the full screen to display the slides and the presentation is self-running. This would usually be used for showing a presentation at an exhibition, or in a shop. Action buttons or hyperlinks are created for the user to move themselves around the presentation.

As we have seen previously, it is not necessary to use PowerPoint as a tool for presenting a slide show. You can use it to create overhead projector transparencies, handouts to support a presentation or 35 mm slides to be shown through a projector (see Chapter 1).

During the course of this book you have discovered how to show a presentation in the most commonly used way, i.e. *Presented by speaker*. Here you can practise changing the view for the two alternate options.

Open an existing presentation, or work through these steps to create a new one.

❶   Create a new presentation, with two slides. The first is to be a title slide and the second a bulleted list.

❷   In the title placeholder of Slide 1 key in:
       Technical Colleges in East Anglia

❸   In Slide 2, type into the title placeholder:
       Selection criteria

❹   In the bulleted list placeholder, type:
       • Courses should meet your specifications
       • Flexibility of tuition and modules
       • Cost

❺   Save the presentation.

Usually you would add effects to the slides as well but for the sake of this exercise we are going to leave the slides as they are.

To set these slides up for an individual to view straight from a computer monitor:

❶   Go to Slide 1.

❷   Open the **Slide Show** menu and select **Set Up Show**.

❸   In the **Show type** box, select *Browsed by an individual*.

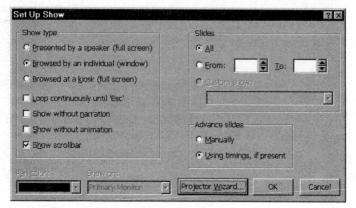

Figure 11.1 The **Set Up Show** dialog box

❹   Click **OK**.

❺   Click on Slide Show view to view the presentation.

When the screen changes to the Slide Show view it contains a Menu bar, and, if it's being shown over the Web, the Web toolbar can be added.

The menus provide the tools for interacting with the presentation.

The **File** menu commands enable users to print, open other presentations, end the show and look at the properties of the presentation – these show its summary contents, author, size and other details.

The **Edit** menu commands enable the viewer to edit the presentation, after returning to the normal screen. Clicking the Slide Show button will return to the presentation after editing. It is also possible to copy a slide in this view using **Copy Slide**.

The **Browse** menu can be used to select a different slide, advance or return through a presentation.

Menu bar   Web toolbar   Scroll bar and slider

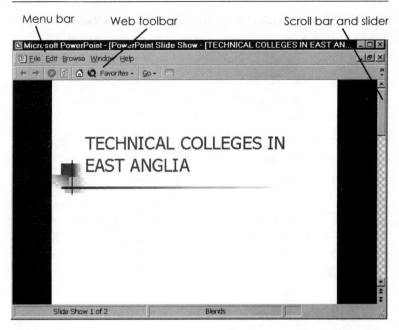

Figure 11.2 A slide show in *Browsed by an individual* view

The **Window** menu lists all open presentations and by clicking on a file name, that presentation will appear on the screen. You can also open or close the Web toolbar here.

The **shortcut** menu, reached through the right mouse button, in this view offers the popular menu options for managing the presentation.

The scroll bars move the operator through the presentation, as do the **[Page Up]** and **[Page Down]** keys.

Now you can set up the same presentation with some effects, set it to be browsed at a kiosk and then run it.

❶ Open the **File** menu and select **End show**.

❷ Having returned to the previous view, open the **Slide Show** menu and select **Custom Animations...** Set up some simple animations and sounds, with timings for each.

❸ Open the **Slide Show** menu and select **Slide Transition...** then set up transition effects between the two slides.

❹ Open the **Slide Show** menu again and select **Rehearse Timings** and record the timings for the full presentation.

❺ Open the **Slide Show** menu again! This time select **Set Up Show...**

❻ Select *Browsed at a kiosk*, tick the **Using timings, if present** option, and click **OK**.

❼ Click the Slide Show view button to view the presentation.

When it comes to the end of the second slide wait for it to loop round back to the beginning and show the presentation again. By default the browsed at a kiosk view is designed to work on a continuous loop. This means that when it has reached the end it will automatically start at the beginning again. It can be stopped by pressing **[Escape]**.

11.2 Self-running presentations

Self-running presentations are an ideal way of creating a presentation which will be viewed on an exhibition stand, in a shop, as part of a college open day, recruitment drive or for other purposes where there will be no-one available to operate it. It can be left unmanned and set with action buttons (see section 11.4) so that the viewer can move forward to the next slide or it can be set on a loop so that as soon as the presentation comes to the end it will restart.

A self-running presentation is created in the same way as any other, using all the same effects and formatting facilities. To set it up to self-run, follow the steps above for a *Browsed at a kiosk* presentation.

11.3 Navigating through slides

When giving a presentation you often find that in a question and answer session at the end, people refer to slides shown 30 minutes earlier and it's useful to be able to bring that slide onto the screen quickly and efficiently to help clarify their point, support your answer or simply make the discussion clearer for other members of the audience. When working in Slide Show view with a presentation *Presented by a speaker* you can return to previous slides by clicking with the right mouse button on the computer screen, and selecting **Go** from the shortcut menu. From the **Go** sub-menu you can select *By title* or *Slide navigator*.

♦   **By title** will list the title of each slide in the presentation and you select the one you wish to view.

♦   **Slide navigator** shows a list of all the slides in the presentation.

Select the one you wish to view, click on **Go to**, or double-click on the slide title.

If you happen to know the number of the slide that is being discussed, for instance, number 3 in the series, press the relevant number key and press **[Enter]**. This will take you directly to that slide.

On occasions when you want to set up the presentation for the viewer to navigate around themselves, as in a self-running presentation you will need to set up hyperlinks or action buttons.

11.4 Hyperlinks

Hyperlinks are commands that link the presentation on the screen to other files or devices. They enable the viewer to navigate themselves around and move to other relevant slides, import a narrative and so on. The viewer can go to a variety of locations and doesn't have to stay within the presentation. By clicking on to a hyperlink button your viewer can go to files in different applications, an Internet site or an e-mail address. A hyperlink can be made up of any object including text, graphs, objects or tables. There are also some predefined hyperlinks available on the Action buttons (see section 11.5).

The text for hyperlinks is in a different colour from the rest of the text. The colour will change after the hyperlink location has been viewed.

Before we can test hyperlinks, we need something to link to.

❶   Create a new presentation consisting of one title slide.

❷   Type in a title – perhaps 'St Peter's Technical College'.

❸   Save and close the slide.

To insert a hyperlink into a presentation:

❶   Return to the two-slide presentation you created earlier. Select the sub-title placeholder of the first slide. To insert a hyperlink, the placeholder or object in a slide to which it relates should always be selected.

❷   Open the **Insert** menu and select **Hyperlink...**.

❸   Type in the **Text to display**, e.g. 'Click here for further information on colleges'.

❹   Select *Existing File or Web Page* in the **Link to** box, then select **recent files**.

❺   From the list, select the name of the new presentation file.

❻   Check the file name has been inserted into the box above the list of files.

❼   Click **OK**.

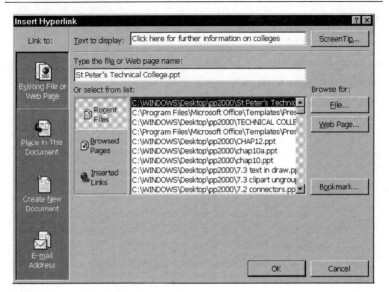

Figure 11.3 Defining a hyperlink

Figure 11.4 A slide containing a hyperlink

You will see now that the Text to display has appeared in the sub-title placeholder in a different colour from the rest of the text.

A hyperlink can also be added to existing text. Select the text before using the Insert – Hyperlink command, then continue as above.

Having set up the hyperlink, it's time to run the presentation:

❶   Click the Slide Show view button to run the presentation.

❷   When the slide with the hyperlink appears, point at the hyperlink with the mouse pointer – now like this 🖑 – and click on it once.

❸   When the link has finished and you want to return to the presentation, press **End show** on the shortcut menu or the action button in the bottom left corner of the Slide Show view. You will then return to the original presentation.

11.5 Action buttons

Action buttons are predesigned hyperlinks already available within PowerPoint. They enable the viewer to move between slides, play movies or sound. The buttons depict shapes that indicate their function, for example:

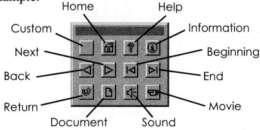

These shapes are all commonly used symbols in terms of multimedia and Internet functions and so should be understood by the viewer. Note that some of these hyperlinks are for navigating between slides, others are for opening sound, movie or document files.

Action buttons are simple to set up. You are now going to add an action button to a slide in this presentation. When clicked, it will play a sound.

❶ Select a practice slide.

❷ Open the **Slide Show** menu.

❸ Point to **Action buttons** and select the *sound* button.

❹ Click onto the slide where you want it to go and drag the button to the size required.

❺ The **Action Setting** dialog box will open automatically. Select a sound from the drop-down **Play sound** list.

Action buttons and hyperlinks can work together so that clicking the action button sets off the hyperlink. You can also set up a hyperlink so that passing the mouse over it will activate it. Here's how:

❶ Select the text, graphic or other item to carry the hyperlink.

❷ Open the **Slide Show** menu and select **Action Settings**.

❸ Click on the **Mouse over** tab and select **Hyperlink to:**, then open the drop-down list and select the target of your hyperlink. Some links will require further definition, e.g. a hyperlink to an URL will need an Internet address. Fill in the details boxes as required.

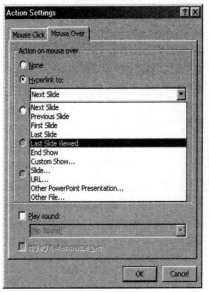

❹ Click **OK**.

11.6 Pack and Go Wizard

Believe it or not it is possible to show a presentation through a computer that does not have PowerPoint installed! Only though, if you've used the Pack and Go Wizard.

A slide show to be presented on another computer needs to be created exactly as you usually would. Insert any effects, sounds, clip art, hyperlinks, etc. that you want to use.

> ◆ Having completed and saved it, open the **File** menu and select **Pack and Go Wizard**. Just follow its steps to save a compressed version of your presentation on to disk. Don't be alarmed if you need more than one disk on which to pack the file.

If the presentation is changed after you have packed it, rerun the wizard and pack it again.

The only thing you must do when using the Pack and Go wizard is to confirm the installation of the PowerPoint Viewer. Without this file you will not be able to run the presentation on a different computer. Check that the disk contains *Ppview32*, the PowerPoint Viewer.

The presentation must be unpacked and loaded onto the host computer.

> ❶ Insert the floppy disk into the computer from which the presentation will be shown.

> ❷ Open Windows Explorer, and select *pngsetup* from the list of files on the floppy disk.

> ❸ In the dialog box which appears, key in a destination folder for the presentation (see Figure 11.5).

> ❹ When it has been loaded successfully, open the destination folder to check that all the files, especially *Ppview32* have loaded successfully.

You can show the presentation immediately by double-clicking on *Ppview32* to view it. In the dialog box (see Figure 11.6) select the name of your presentation (note that it will not have a PowerPoint icon

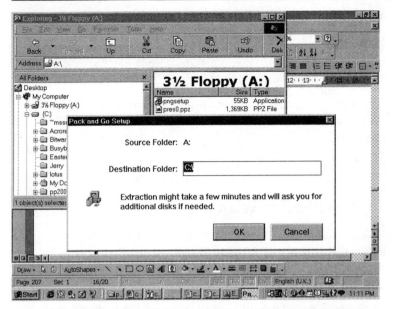

Figure 11.5 Unpacking the presentation on the target computer

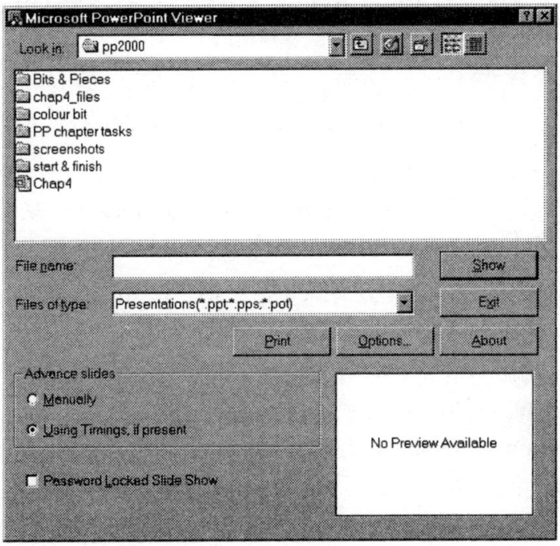

Figure 11.6 The Ppview32 (PowerPoint Viewer) dialog box

alongside the file name) and click on **Show**. Your presentation will run just as it would on the computer from which it was copied.

♦ When using the Pack and Go Wizard it is not necessary to be working in the presentation to be packed up but you must be in *a* presentation.

If you want to show the presentation at a later time, open the destination folder on the host computer, either through My Computer or Windows Explorer, double-click on *Ppview32* and load the presentation file as above.

11.7 Projector Wizard

When running a slide show on a computer that is attached to a projector for the first time you must ensure you have worked through the Projector Wizard. This takes your computer through the steps of locating and installing the new hardware.

Before running the wizard connect the computer to the projector.

❶ Open the **Slide Show** menu and open **Set Up Show**. Click the **Projector Wizard** button.

❷ The wizard will give you step-by-step instructions for setting it up to work with the project to which it is connected.

With Windows 98 it is possible to run the presentation on two monitors (assuming you have dual-monitor hardware installed). One monitor will show the slide show and the other can be used to view the slides, notes and outline.

11.8 Note-taking during a presentation

This facility is particularly useful if the presentation is being made to a small group of people, either all viewing one monitor, or participating in an on-line meeting. If it is being made to a large audience, such as a lecture then it wouldn't necessarily be very useful, although it's still worth familiarizing yourself with it.

Whilst running a presentation you can open **Meeting minder** or **Speaker notes** on to the screen by clicking with the right mouse button and selecting either from the shortcut menu. They enable you to take notes as the meeting is progressing. Be aware though, the notes, when being made during an on-line meeting can be seen by all the participants.

Figure 11.7 Meeting Minder, after Export has been clicked to open its dialog box

If you select **Speaker notes** through the shortcut menu, you will be able to read any existing notes for that slide and add extra notes.

By selecting **Meeting Minder** and the **Meeting Minutes** tab, you can make notes of the presentation. If action is to be taken following the presentation this information can be added into the **Action Items** tab. You can export these to Word so that they can be edited and formatted as a full report or minutes of the meeting, or to Outlook for forwarding on to those to take action.

Simply type in the notes, move to the **Action** tab to add any action items if needed and click on **Export** button. In the Export dialog box (see Figure 11.7), tick the box that the notes and action should be exported to, then click **Export Now**.

Those action items that have been forwarded to Outlook will be on its Task list and can be forwarded from there to the recipient. Anything forwarded to Word will be brought up on your screen.

SUMMARY

In this chapter we have discussed the following:

✓ Presenting a slide show through a variety of media.

✓ Using Action buttons to play sounds or activate hyperlinks.

✓ Copying a presentation to another computer with the
Pack and Go Wizard.

✓ Using the Projector Wizard to configure a projector for
a presentation.

✓ Taking notes during a presentation.

12 USEFUL TIPS

12.1 Adding and customizing toolbars

To speed up the use of Microsoft applications, including PowerPoint, you can display toolbars for every function or customize toolbars so that they contain the buttons you use most frequently. One click on a button replaces the process of opening and selecting from a menu.

To load toolbars that are not currently displayed:

❶ Point the mouse at the menu bar or a space on a toolbar (don't point at a button).

❷ Click with the right mouse button.

❸ Click, with the left button, on any other toolbars that you would like to have up on your screen.

To customize a toolbar:

❶ Point the mouse at the menu bar or a space on a toolbar.

❷ Right-click and select the **Customize...** option at the bottom of the menu. This opens a dialog box with three tabs.

❸ Bring the **Commands** tab to the front.

❹ Select the **Category** that contains the command you want to place on the toolbars, e.g. *Insert*.

❺ From the Commands list, choose the button you want, e.g. *Organization Chart*, and drag it onto one of the toolbars.

❼ Click **Close**.

Figure 12.1 The **Customize** dialog box

TOOLBAR ICONS AND LABELS

The icon by the side of a command name becomes the toolbar button. If a command does not have an icon, its name will be used to label a button for the toolbar, e.g. the **Record Sound** command becomes the ⬚Record Sound⬚ button.

To remove a button from a toolbar:

❶ Open the **Customize** dialog box as above.

❷ Drag the button from the toolbar to anywhere inside the dialog box.

12.2 Using slides from other presentations

Why reproduce slides each time you create a new presentation if they already exist somewhere else, or if something similar already exists?

You can very easily import slides from one presentation to another and insert it as it is or, once it's in the new presentation, manipulate it and format it to meet the needs of the new presentation:

❶ Show the slide that will come before the one you're going to insert.

❷ Open the **Insert** menu, select **Slides from Files**.

❸ Find the presentation from which you want to copy a slide.

❹ Click **Display**.

❺ Select the slides to be copied and click **Insert**.

❻ To copy the whole presentation, click **Insert All**.

12.3 Creating your own templates

We have discussed earlier in the book using predesigned templates or wizards for your presentations. You might, though, feel that it would be useful for every presentation you do to contain standard corporate colours, or slogans, fonts, etc. This can be achieved by setting up the Slide Master for each presentation to ensure continuity through a presentation (see Chapter 2). Alternatively, it would be quicker for you to take the time to set up a Slide Master and Title Master and save them in one file as a template, a copy of which can then be accessed every time you need it.

For instance, if you want to create a template for new business presentations you might feel that it would be a good idea to have the same colour scheme, the company logo, and a particular font used throughout.

❶ Open PowerPoint to create a new presentation. Select any option at the **New Slide** dialog box (as you are going to set up a Slide Master, it doesn't matter which you select).

❷ Open the **View** menu, point to **Master** and select **Slide Master**.

❸ Format the Slide Master to meet your requirements

❹ Open the **Insert** menu, and select **New Title Master**.

❺ Format this slide following the guidelines in Chapter 5.

❻ Open the **File** menu, and select **Save As**.

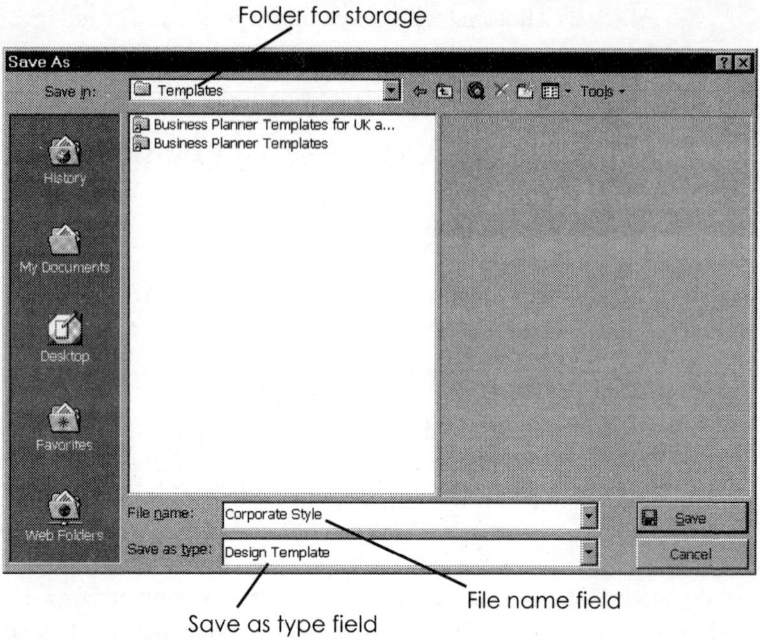

Folder for storage

Save as type field   File name field

Figure 12.2 The **Save As** dialog box when saving a template

❼ In the **Save as type** field, select *Design Template*.

You'll notice that the **Save in** box now shows that you are going to save it into the templates folder.

❽ Key in a name for the template, e.g. *corporate style*.

❾ Click **Save**.

To use the template (with PowerPoint already open)

❶ Open the **File** menu and select **New**.

❷ From the **New presentation** dialog box select your template from within the **General** tab.

❸ Click **OK**.

To open a template when loading PowerPoint:

❶ Start PowerPoint in the usual way.

❷ Select **Design Template**.

❸ Go to the **General** tab and select your template.

❹ Click on **OK**.

◆ If the template opens showing Title Master or Slide Master, click onto one of the View buttons, e.g. Normal view, to get to a normal working screen.

You may add extra slides to the presentation by using the **New Slide** option in the **Insert** menu.

12.4 Using the Office Assistant

Microsoft has produced an on-screen 'assistant' to help you through more difficult or complicated moments whilst using one of the Office suite applications. This is called the Office Assistant, and will probably appear as a paperclip but it can take on many different forms!

To access the Office Assistant, if it's not already visible on your screen, click on the **Help** button [?] on the standard toolbar. It will then appear, with a speech bubble into which you can type in your question.

Having keyed in your question, click **Search** and the related topics in the Help system will be listed on your screen. Find the topic you require and click on it for more details.

What would you like to do?

❷ Hide a slide in a slide show

❷ Change a slide so that it differs from the slide master

❷ Display a hidden slide during a slide show

❷ Display or hide multiple presentations on the Windows taskbar

❷ Display or hide the File menu list of recently used presentations

▼ See more...

How do I hide slides?

Options   Search

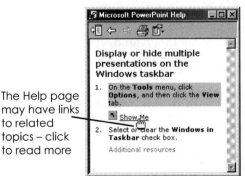

The Help page may have links to related topics – click to read more

🛂 Microsoft PowerPoint Help

Display or hide multiple presentations on the Windows taskbar

1. On the **Tools** menu, click **Options**, and then click the **View** tab.

   ◻ Show Me

2. Select or clear the **Windows in Taskbar** check box.

   Additional resources

If you click on the **Options** button, you open the dialog box enabling you to change your Office Assistant to a different character, such as The Dot, The Genius, the Office Logo, Mother Nature, Links or Rocky.

If you prefer to work without the Office Assistant, you can turn it off by right-clicking on it and selecting **Hide**.

12.5 Keyboard commands

We have concentrated on using the mouse, menu and toolbar commands to create slides. It is, however, quite possible to operate PowerPoint with the keyboard commands. The majority of these are the same throughout all Microsoft applications; the ones listed here are specific to PowerPoint.

Designing presentations

Function	**Key**
Create a new presentation	**[Control] + [N]**
Insert a new slide	**[Control] + [M]**
Copy a slide	**[Control] + [D]**
Open a presentation	**[Control] + [O]**
Close a presentation	**[Control] + [W]**
Print a presentation	**[Control] + [P]**
Save a presentation	**[Control] + [S]**
Run a presentation	**[F5]**
Search and find	**[Control] + [F]**
Search and replace	**[Control] + [H]**
Insert a hyperlink	**[Control] + [K]**
Check spelling	**[F7]**
Undo last action	**[Control] + [Z]**
Redo last action	**[Control] + [Y]**
Move to the next pane	**[F6]**
Move to the previous pane	**[Shift] + [F6]**

Working with outlines

Function	Key
Promote a paragraph	**[Alt]** + **[Shift]** + **[←]**
Demote a paragraph	**[Alt]** + **[Shift]** + **[→]**
Move selected paragraphs up	**[Alt]** + **[Shift]** + **[↑]**
Move selected paragraphs down	**[Alt]** + **[Shift]** + **[↓]**
Show heading level 1	**[Alt]** + **[Shift]** + **[1]**
Expand text below a heading	**[Alt]** + **[Shift]** + **[+]**
Collapse text below a heading	**[Alt]** + **[Shift]** + **[–]**
Show all text or headings	**[Alt]** + **[Shift]** + **[A]**

Slide shows

Function	Key
Move to next animation or slide	**[N]**, **[Enter]**, **[Pg Dn]**, **[→]**, **[↓]** or **[Spacebar]**
Return to the previous animation or slide	**[P]**, **[Pg Up]**, **[←]**, **[→]** or **[Backspace]**
Go to slide number …	Type number and **[Enter]**
Display a black screen	**[B]**
Display a white screen	**[W]**
Stop or restart an automatic slide show	**[S]**
End a slide show	**[Esc]**
Move to next hidden slide	**[H]**
Change new timings during rehearsal	**[T]**
Show mouse pointer	**[Control]** + **[P]** or + **[A]**
Change the pointer to a pen	**[Control]** + **[P]**
Change the pointer back to an arrow	**[Control]** + **[A]**
Hide the mouse pointer	**[Control]** + **[H]**
Hide the mouse pointer after 15 seconds	**[Control]** + **[U]**
Open the shortcut menu	**[Shift]** + **[F10]**
Go to the next hyperlink	**[Tab]**

Go to the previous hyperlink	**[Shift]** + **[Tab]**
Activate a hyperlink	Select then **[Enter]**
Activate mouse over on a hyperlink	Select then **[Shift]** + **[Enter]**

Working with objects

Function	**Key**
Select an object	**[Tab]**or **[Shift]** + **[Tab]**
Select text within a selected object	**[Enter]**
Select all objects/slides	**[Control]** + **[A]**
Open AutoShape menu	**[Alt]** + **[U]**

PRACTICE PROJECTS

Practice Project One

Imagine you are the Hospitality Officer for a large hospital and you have been asked to do a presentation to all the new student doctors. The purpose is to explain the layout of the main hospital building, the regulations that apply to all staff in terms of using the building, facilities available to staff and where to go and what to do should there be a hospitality or maintenance problem.

The presentation should not run for more than 15 minutes including question and answers (as this is only one part of a whole induction day for these new doctors) and should include maximum of 12 lively, fast moving slides. This should also be designed so that there is a link to a Web site.

Step 1

Plan the basis of your presentation on paper so that you've got an idea of what each slide should contain and the graphics, sounds or effects you require.

Step 2   Chapters 1 and 2

Create a new presentation and select the type of presentation format you wish to use, blank slide, template or AutoContent Wizard.

Step 3   Chapters 2, 5–10

Set up your first slide, probably as a title slide and then select nine others to suit the layout that you have planned.

You might feel, for this size of presentation that it's worth setting up the Master Slide so that the colour scheme and basics of each slide are consistent with each other.

Now work through your slides adding in the text and graphics as you want them.

Don't forget you can paste, or paste link from other files if needs be.

- ◆ I would definitely put in transition effects between the slides and would include some sort of sound effect at stages throughout it. There doesn't need to be music behind the presentation because you will be speaking through each slide, to reinforce, and expand on, their content.

Create a set of web pages from the slide show.

The colour section of this book gives examples of the slides created by the author for this project. They were created using skills from chapters from this book and so will demonstrate how everything comes together. Keep in mind that sound effects were also used but unfortunately don't come across in photographs!

Practice Project Two

Imagine you have been asked to put together a presentation to the sales force of your company showing the marketing strategy for next year. The sales team are particularly good, very young and vibrant. Your presentation, therefore, needs to keep their attention and get your point across to them. It is suggested that you have no more than eight slides.

GLOSSARY

Action buttons Predesigned buttons which are inserted on to slides to aid the viewer's movement around the presentation.

Adjustment handle Diamond shaped handle on an object to adjust its shape.

Animated effects Active introduction of objects and text into a slide during the show.

Animated transitions Active movement from one slide to another.

Autocontent Wizard Wizard used to create a full presentation. All you would need to do is add in the text and objects.

Autoshape Menu of shapes in the Drawing toolbar.

Background printing Enables you to continue working on a presentation whilst it, or something else is printing.

Border Lines framing around a placeholder or object.

Broadcast To show your presentation over the Internet to an invited audience. It will not be interactive.

Browsed at kiosk A way of showing a presentation so that it is self-running.

Cell Box which contains values in Graph 2000.

Chat Facility in NetMeeting used by participants of a meeting to communication with each other.

Collaboration Controlled by the host of on-line meetings, it allows all participants to be actively involved.

Connectors Lines used in diagrams to connect objects.

Datasheet The window in Graph 2000 which contains the data from which the graph will be made.

Destination file	The file to which text or objects copied or cut from another file have been pasted.
Dialog box	The window containing the commands or options for the function being performed.
Drawing objects	Lines, shapes, etc. for creating graphics.
Embedded objects	Term given when an object or text has been copied or cut from another file and it has become part of the destination file.
Footers	Space below margins for information such as slide number, date and reference.
Freeform	Drawing tool used to draw lines freehand.
Grid lines	Invisible lines which control positioning, or resizing of objects or placeholders.
Group	Join a number of small objects or graphics together to make them one.
Handles	Blocks around placeholders and objects which are dragged in or out to resize them.
HTML	Hypertext Mark-Up Language, used to create Web pages.
Hyperlink	Link which, when activated, will take the viewer to somewhere else in the presentation, or another location, e.g. another file or Web site.
Indent marker	Arrow head on the ruler used to indent the text from the left.
Insertion point	The vertical flashing bar which indicates where text can be typed.
Legend	Key to the data in a graph
Linked object	Data copied from a source file, but retaining a link to it. When the data in the original file changes so will the data in the destination file.
Margins	Space around the working area of the slide.
Master Slide	A slide used to establish standard colour and layout settings for the whole presentation.

Meeting Minder	Facility for making notes of a meeting whilst it is on going. These notes can be e-mailed to all participants directly from Meeting Minder.
Nudge	To move an object minimally.
Office Assistant	Friendly front-end to the Help system.
Order	Drawing tool which enables you to change the order in which objects overlap.
Organization Chart	An application used to create charts.
Orientation	The way the page is set, i.e. tall (portrait) or wide (landscape).
Pack & Go Wizard	A wizard used to pack up the presentation on to floppy disk and show it using another computer which doesn't have PowerPoint.
Page setup	Used to change the page settings and orientation.
Pane	Section of a window, for instance in Normal view there is the Outline pane, the Slide pane and the Notes pane.
Paste Link	To paste something into a file which is still linked to another file.
Placeholder	Frame or box which contains text and objects.
Points	A unit of measurement for fonts.
PowerPoint viewer	This is the file used to run a presentation on a computer that doesn't have PowerPoint loaded.
Projector Wizard	Used to detect the hardware before showing a presentation through a projector.
Regroup	To bring objects that were grouped and then ungrouped back together.
Rehearse timings	Enables you to rehears the presentation recording the timings so that these can then be used as the timings in the 'real thing'.
Ruler	Can be displayed along the top of the slide for helping with sizing objects or placeholders.

Scroll bar	The bar down the right-hand side of the screen. It is used to move to the next or previous slide.
Select	To click on a placeholder or object, or highlight text, to select it.
Shortcut menu	The menu that will open when the right mouse button is pressed.
Slide colour scheme	The colour scheme given to individual slides or the whole series.
Slide Navigator	Facility to move to specific slides.
Source file	File from which copied or cut text or objects have been taken.
Templates	Predesigned presentations providing colour schemes, font settings and layouts for single slides or for for full presentations.
Text anchor point	Facility on the Drawing toolbar to adjust the fit of text within an object.
Timings	The delay between slides coming on to the screen or projector.
Transition	The way one slides leads into another.
Ungroup	To separate objects that have been previously grouped together.
URL	Uniform Resource Locator, in other words the address of your Web page.
Web site	A set of linked pages on the World Wide Web.
Whiteboard	A facility in NetMeeting used by participants to add text or objects for discussion.
Wizard	A tool that will do the work for you!
Zoom	To increase the size of the slide on the screen so that you can see a larger version of a specific area

INDEX